A Love Story

How the Heartland Fell in Love with a 400-Year-Old French Comedic Playwright

by Chantal M. Roberts

Limit of Liability/Disclaimer of Warranty

This publication is designed to provide accurate and authoritative information regarding the subject matter covered. It is sold with the understanding that the publisher and the author assume no responsibility for errors, inaccuracies, omissions, or any other inconsistencies herein. This publication is meant as a source of valuable information for the reader.

While the publisher and author have used their best efforts in preparing this book, they were in some cases unable to obtain a person's permission to have his or her photographic likeness used. The publisher and author, therefore, decided to use photographs published on social media platforms, on KC MOlière: 400 in 2022's website, and its newsletter. Neither the publisher nor the author shall be liable for any loss of profit or any other commercial damages, including but not limited to special, incidental, consequential, personal, or other damages from the use of these photographs.

Some names and identifying details of people described in this book have been altered to protect their privacy.

The opinions expressed in this book are those of the author.

Indemnity

You agree to defend, indemnify, and hold harmless the author, the publisher, and the copyright holder(s) from and against all the liabilities, claims, damages, and expenses (including reasonable attorney's fees and costs) arising out of your use of this material; your breach or alleged breach of this agreement; or your breach or alleged breach of the copyright, trademark, proprietary or other rights of the author or copyright holder(s).

ISBN: 978-1-7374268-3-7 (paperback)
       978-1-7374268-4-4 (ebook)

For information, please contact:
Chantal M. Roberts, CPCU, AIC, RPA
Tilting at Windmills Press
P.O. Box 4676
Olathe, KS 66213
editor@tiltingatwindmillspress.com

Book cover design by Chantal M. Roberts
Interior design by Laura Orsini, Panoply Publishing LLC

Dedication

To Molière.
Keep doing you.

"It infuriates me to be wrong when I know I'm right."
— Molière

Table of Contents

Introduction

When Felicia approached me to write the history of our organization—and to perhaps offer it as a cautionary tale to others who might also want to begin a festival of their own—I was flattered. I won't say I jumped at the chance, because I remember thinking that it would be difficult. Ultimately, I took the opportunity the Board offered me because it was a different challenge.

I started at the beginning, as any good accounting does, but immediately the history of **KC MOlière: 400 in 2022** began to lend itself to a narrative history, especially since I was tasked with detailing the "trials and tribulations" the organization went through so that others might, possibly, learn from our mistakes. While these misfortunes were largely physical impediments, they had an emotional impact on the people involved, and ultimately, that is what makes history more interesting than dry, boring dates. However, if dates are your thing, I have included a Chronology of Accomplishments at the end of the book.

This is not a tell-all tale; I have admittedly glossed over some issues. I also couldn't write in detail about everyone's efforts—such as the Fundraising Committee, which barely makes a cameo in the book. This is not to belittle their work; if anything, they were one of the most essential committees whose work made the whole event possible. Indeed, if it hadn't been for them and their efforts, we likely would not have obtained sponsors, grants, and the money necessary to commission works.

I have also used the final forms of projects throughout the book to avoid confusion. For example, our name and coloring were originally **KC MOlière: 400 in 2022** to bring to mind the bleu, blanc, rouge (blue, white, red) of the French flag; somewhere along the way (no one can remember why), it was changed to the current form: **KC MOlière: 400 in 2022**. Therefore, in the book, you will see the final version, as opposed to the first iteration from the original document.

Although I've fashioned this recounting as more of a story, I have taken great pains to not to take too much artistic license. I, unfortunately, was not able to interview everyone involved in the project—perhaps another time—so those who were involved might have a different memory or feeling than what I attributed to them. I ask your indulgence. I've also attempted to not focus on myself too much.

I refer to myself in the third person because this is not my story; I am merely a supporting cast member.

Events may be taken slightly out of order for the sake of the story. Jumping around in time happens often in fiction, and while this is nonfiction, I feel the flow works better and that readers won't be confused.

Finally, I would like to thank the Board of **KC MOlière: 400 in 2022** for the faith they have shown in me; I sincerely hope they like this recounting.

Merci: Felicia, Don, Jim, Pat, Becky, Jennifer, Dorothée, and Cyprienne.

The author would also like to thank (in no particular order):

Venne-Richard Londré

Don Ipock

Julián Zugazagoitia

Doug Frost

Frédéric Gasnier

Catherine Tissot

KC *Studio Magazine*

Katheryn E. Bilbo

Nicole Marie Green

Calan Welder

Fred Homan

Amanda Davison

Aaron Roberts

David Weber

Jérôme Pouly

KC Studio

David MacCay

Cie Coeur et Panache

Paul Gutiérrez

Martin Cizmar

Richard Rischar

John Rice

Georgiana Londré Buchanan

Catherine Rush-Thompson

René Bollier

Suzanne Kinner

Nathalie Feldman

Jennifer Martin

IN Kansas City

Stephanie Roberts

MoMo

Margaret Shelby

KC MOlière: 400 in 2022's first administrative assistant
and second assistant, Alexia Lamb.

KC MOlière: 400 in 2022 Committee Chairs

Danielle Trebus & Martin English
Education K-12

Jennifer Martin & Mechele Leon
Education Colleges and Universities

Don Dagenais
Fundraising and Financial

Cyprienne Simchowitz
International Relations

**Cynthia Levin &
Damron Russel Armstrong**
Thoroughly Modern Molière

**Linda Ade Brand &
Tracy Terstriep Herber**
Cultural Context Music and Dance

**Trudie Homan &
Beth Byrd-Lonski**
Cultural Context Visual & Popular
Arts

**Georgianna Buchanan &
Claire Davis**
Social

Catherine Tissot
President, Alliance Française
de Kansas City

Dorothée Werner
Académie Lafayette Liaison

Linda Williams
KC Melting Pot Theatre Liaison

Stephanie Roberts
UMKC Liaison and Director
of Mobile Molière

**John Rensenhouse & Sidonie
Garrett**
Honorary Theatrical Liaison

**Patricia Hamarstrom Williams &
Rebecca Smith**
Press and Publications

Chantal Roberts
Website Events Editor, Newsletter
Editor, Book Club Convener

Catherine Rush Thompson
Website Blog/*Jeu de Plume* Editor

C'est une histoire d'amour
This Is a Love Story

Like any good, classical love story, there is a boy and a girl. The world conspires to keep them from one another. They are oceans apart. There are tragedies. There are glimpses of hope, only to be dashed again. Sometimes the boy and girl don't even speak the same language.

Except the language of love. And theatre.

And maybe there are a few presumptuous servants to keep the story moving along.

This is the story of the Kansas Citians who overcame the untimely deaths of two giants chaperoning the meeting of the lovers, a world that didn't understand them, and the pandemic which nearly undid them. This is a love story about people in Kansas City who fell in love with Molière, a French comedic playwright.

This is the story of two flyover states in the Heartland opening their arms to welcome the genius that is Molière.

In Celebration!

French playwright Molière was born on 15 January 1622. Two hundred years later, Kansas City became a French settlement and Missouri became a state. Celebrations of the 400th birthday and the 200th anniversary came together in the 2021/22 theatre season and in city-wide arts events: **KC Molière: 400 in 2022**.

Why Kansas City?

François Chouteau settled at the confluence of the Kansas and Missouri rivers and opened a fur-trading post where French families interacted with Osage and Kansa natives.

A significant milestone in the region's historic linkage to France is marked by the 2021 Missouri Bicentennial celebration of the operation of the Chouteau Trading Post on the banks of the Missouri River and the founding of Kansas City, Missouri. July 2021 witnessed the unveiling of sculptures of Chouteau and two Osage natives atop the François Chouteau and Native American Heritage Fountain and the KC Molière commissioned play, *Tartuffenthrope!*

Molière's comedies have always been part of Kansas City's vibrant theatre scene. Demographically, Kansas City ranks in the top three American cities for support of the arts.

With ten professional theatre companies, as well as many semi-professional companies, Kansas City's annual per capita theatre attendance is one of the highest in the nation. Most of these organizations are devoted to English-language works of the last quarter century, which means that the next generation is largely deprived of exposure to classics other than Shakespeare. Despite the quantity of theatrical activity, there is almost never a foreign play in translation.

The Heartland

Kansas City's geographical location in the middle of the USA, in what is known as "flyover country," means that the accomplishments of our artists tend to be overlooked. Critics from the American East and West coasts don't cover our original works as they do up and down both coasts.

Being in the heart of the country and encompassing a fourteen-county metropolitan area offered the perfect locale for celebrating a 400-year-old French comedic playwright.

Afterall, Molière, like any Frenchman, always wrote about love.

Célébrons!

Molière est né le 15 janvier 1622. Deux cents ans plus tard, les premiers habitants français fondèrent ce qui allait devenir Kansas City et l'état du Missouri naquit. La ville célèbrerait ces 400ème et 200ème anniversaires en même temps lors de la saison théâtrale 2021-22 ainsi qu'avec des manifestations artistiques dans toute la ville: **KC MOlière: 400 in 2022**.

Pourquoi Kansas City?

François Chouteau s'établit au confluent des fleuves Kansas et Missouri et ouvrit un poste de traite de fourrures où les familles françaises et les tribus locales Osage et Kansa pouvaient se rencontrer.

Une étape importante dans le lien historique de la région avec la France est marquée par la célébration du bicentenaire du Missouri en 2021 de l'exploitation du Chouteau Trading Post sur les rives du fleuve Missouri et la fondation de Kansas City, Missouri. Juillet 2021 a été témoin du dévoilement des sculptures de Chouteau et de deux indigènes Osage au sommet de la fontaine du patrimoine François Chouteau et amérindien et de la pièce de théâtre commandée par KC MOlière, « Tartuffenthrope! »

Les pièces de Molière ont depuis toujours fait partie de la vibrante scène théâtrale de Kansas City. Part rapport à sa population elle figure parmi les trois premières villes des États-Unis pour le soutien aux arts.

Avec dix compagnies de théâtre professionnelles ainsi que de nombreuses compagnies semi-professionnelles, la fréquentation annuelle du théâtre par habitant est l'une des plus élevées du pays. La plupart de ces organisations se consacrent aux œuvres de langue anglaise du dernier quart de siècle, ce qui signifie que la prochaine génération est largement privée d'exposition à des classiques autres que Shakespeare. Malgré la quantité d'activité théâtrale, il n'y a presque jamais de pièce étrangère en traduction.

Le cœur du pays

La situation géographique de Kansas City au milieu des États-Unis, dans ce que l'on appelle le « pays survolé », signifie que les réalisations de nos artistes ont tendance à être négligées. Les critiques des côtes est et ouest américaines ne couvrent pas nos œuvres originales comme elles le font le long des deux côtes.

Être au cœur du pays et englobant une zone métropolitaine de quatorze comtés offrait un lieu idéal pour célébrer un dramaturge comique français âgé de 400 ans.

Après tout, Molière, comme tout Français, a toujours écrit sur l'amour.

L'Idée
The Idea

"Did you know Molière will be 400 in four years?" Felicia Londré, a ceaseless ball of energy and a Curators' Distinguished Professor of Theatre at the University of Missouri–Kansas City, mentioned to her friend, Kip Niven. The house lights were up, but it was still dim backstage as the audience trickled out of the theatre. Felicia's eyes adjusted to the darkness. She and her husband, Venne, had just attended Kip's EARTh (Equity Actors Reading Theatre) reading of *Le Médecin malgré lui* (*The Doctor in Spite of Himself*).

By virtue of her clout in the Kansas City theatre scene, Felicia had permanent backstage access after a show. Venne held their coats, ready for a chilly walk back to their car in the December night air.

Kip, for his part, was a handsome Kansas City native, a successful actor who'd starred in various television shows like *The Waltons*, *Alice*, *All My Children*, and *Walker, Texas Ranger*, but his real claim to fame was *Magnum Force*, the 1973 Dirty Harry movie, playing Officer Astrachan. Twelve months prior to Kip's reading, in January 2017, Felicia submitted a proposal to four Kansas City artistic directors alerting them to… well, a once-in-400 years opportunity. The idea—to have a city-wide *fête* combining all the arts, à la the Actors Theatre of Louisville's Humana Festival which involved various Louisville arts organizations and had a different cultural theme each year, and by the long-ago Midwest Shakespeare Chautauqua in 1980 —died with barely a whimper, despite her plea to "grab onto this important 400th anniversary Molière milestone and make a huge splash with it."

Felicia sighed in acquiescence, resigning herself to the fact that if the theatres most likely to produce Molière's works weren't behind her, more peripheral related events, such as museum exhibits, university lectures, ballets, operas, and orchestras would be unlikely to pick up the banner.

Like children the night before Christmas, visions of an ambitious, international celebration of France's—indeed, the world's—greatest comedic dramatist danced in Felicia's head, with months-long exhibits, music concerts, and erudite lectures. Alas, this star-crossed love affair had a fundamental drawback. No one outside of high school/college French class and/or the theatre knew who Molière was. After all, Shakespeare wrote great comedies *and* tragedies, and there are dozens of annual Shakespeare festivals. No one needed or wanted more classical plays, especially in a foreign language.

No, the arranged marriage between America and Shakespeare had been cemented, the contract signed by the short-sighted "culture vultures"; it mattered not that a feisty woman in a flyover state conceived of a dazzling, international cultural event resplendent with glitterati.

Unfortunately for the cultural matchmakers, Molière always had meddling servants, who were much wiser and craftier than the main characters. These servants helped Molière achieve his perpetual goal of happily ever after. One of them stomped into Felicia's office during Spring Break in March 2018, quickly followed by the other the same summer.

Le valet et la bonne
The Valet and the Maid

Spring 2018 reneged on her promise of warmer temperatures and instead offered plummeting days with a strong, northerly wind as Kip rounded the corner to Felicia's office in the James C. Olsen Performing Arts Center. It was a miserable way to spend Spring Break, Kip considered. His fingers were beginning to thaw out from the short jaunt between the car and building.

"We're going to celebrate Molière's birthday," he declared.

Felicia, preoccupied with teaching and other academic business, blinked at Kip's non-sequitur and sudden appearance in her doorway. Had he just shown up, or did they have an appointment she'd forgotten? Regardless, she was grateful that Kip hadn't let up on her idea of a citywide festival. He was constantly emailing her, asking to meet.

"We are going to gather professionals with expertise in coordinating and mounting a festival. But first, we must have a meeting. When does school end?"

"Early May."

"Excellent. Let's do this: the industry is off on Monday. How's Monday, May 21?" Kip didn't wait for a reply. "We invite Jerry Harrington from the Tivoli Theatre, John Rensenhouse, Cynthia from the Unicorn…We'll need some press to cover this. Who do you know?"

Felicia had a tell that belied her age. A small jump in her seat when she was excited—she was five again on Christmas Day, unable to keep still and quiet until Mom and Dad woke up so they could open presents.

"Becky Smith is from *KC Studio*. She is very active in the arts scene, as well. She'll likely write an article."

"We should invite Cyprienne; she's the Honorary French Consul for this area,"

Kip lowered his voice. "I want to get her on our side. She's told the Consulat Général's Chicago office about our initiative, but I don't want them stealing our thunder!" Kip's elocution was a thing of beauty; his voice rose toward the end as a call to action.

"We shouldn't forget the Alliance Française and Academie Layfayette. We can have it here, at UMKC. I'll ask Calan to take minutes. What about Patrick from Commedia Kansas City, since Molière used *commedia dell'arte*, and Beth?" Felicia began tentatively, though following Kip's lead, her voice picked up speed as her thoughts tumbled out of her mouth.

"Well, it's decided," smiled Kip. "We're going to have a party."

L to R: Felicia and Kip enjoy a bottle or two of wine at the 21 May 2018 Molière Anniversary Event First Meeting. (Photo: Calan Welder)

"You like vintage, don't you?" the realtor asked. "You should go to Retro Inferno. It's on Grand in KCMO. Lots of mid-century furniture. I spend entirely too much when I'm there. My house is filled to the rafters!"

Aaron and Chantal Roberts had signed the mortgage paperwork on Tuesday, July 10, 2018, cementing their hasty move to the Kansas City metro area.

"That would be good to check out; get to know our town a bit better," Chantal suggested.

Four days later, Chantal, spying a local arts magazine positioned by Retro Inferno's exit, grabbed it. Those publications were always good for finding something to do, somewhere to volunteer. And so, Chantal's logic went, if you were volunteering at something, the other people volunteering must like it, too, so you'd have a ready-made bond, which should make it easier to make friends, right? Because it just sucks to have to start over with making friends, she thought.

They were on their way home, her husband driving as usual, Chantal flipping through the magazine, when her eyes stopped on page 22.

This was it.

Chantal loved live theatre. It amazed her that actors, costumes, and lights could take an empty space and create an entire world where everything else ceased to exist for several hours.

And *Molière*.

Well. There's simply no comparison. She'd worshipped at the altar of Molière since 10th grade French class with Madame Mistrict.

ARTS IN BRIEF

MOLIÈRE FESTIVAL TO CELEBRATE THE PLAYWRIGHT'S 400TH BIRTHDAY

Kansas City loves its festivals, and there's a new one in the works.

Plans are underway for a possibly year-long festival celebrating the 400th birthday of master French playwright Molière in 2022. That's four years away, but a group of community arts leaders has already begun confabbing on the idea.

Molière

UMKC Theater Professor and renowned historian Felicia Londre and well-known KC actor Kip Niven are spearheading the project. There are reasons Kansas City qualifies as a suitable site for the festival, including its growing recognition as a top-notch theater town. The city boasts a wealth of theater talent, a booming number of theater companies and premieres, and strong college theater departments.

And there is this: Kansas City's origins are French. Alors! KC began as the Chouteau Trading Post of French fur traders 200 years after Molière; a Francois Chouteau Native American Fountain in the Northland is to be completed by 2022. The city's major landowner in the mid-1800s was French; Sarah Bernhardt (French), performed here on five of her nine American tours. More recently, the high-profile exchanges between the Nelson-Atkins Museum of Art and museums in Paris, with the Picasso and the Plains Indians exhibitions, have given KC a degree of prestige in France.

Molière's message remains timely. Though often comedic, his plays were incisive; his greatest strength was pinpointing the hypocrisy in society, particularly among the dominant class. "The Huntington Theatre Company's 'Tartuffe' has one foot in 1664, the other in Trump Tower," a reviewer wrote of the play's 2017 production in Boston.

Molière's work encompassed not just theater, but music, dance, visual arts, literature and costuming. And the festival plans to reflect that breadth. Plays, ballets, operas, puppet shows, library events, movies, school workshops, museum offerings, book groups and more will showcase Molière's comic genius. Merchandise is also being planned.

Stay tuned as this Joie de Molière takes shape. Kansas City may rekindle its reputation as the "Paris of the Plains."
— Rebecca Smith

Reprinted with the kind permission of KC Studio.

"And there is going to be a *festival*. Dedicated to Molière. I mean, can it be *any more* perfect?" she gushed to her husband. She may have actually squealed like a little girl, she was so enthralled with the idea.

The first thing Chantal did on Monday, July 16, 2018—her fourth day, and first full week at her new job—was Google "UMKC Theatre Professor and renowned historian Felicia Londré."

It was easier for Chantal to email Felicia. She could sound like a complete lunatic. "Um, hi. I have loved Molière since 10th grade French class. Can I be your friend?"

Actors are probably frightened of complete lunatics because... stalker, much? So, theatre professors, who were doubtless more accustomed to awkward, weird people, were really a safer bet, Chantal concluded, as she pressed send on the email to Felicia.

Following in Kip's footsteps without even realizing it, Chantal navigated the university campus to find out how she could help. Felicia's office amused Chantal, striking her as the prototypical professor's office. Books were crammed onto bookshelves lining three of the four walls. Books and playbills lay on both chairs in front of Felicia's fake wood desk, the kind you might have seen a secretary from the 1980s using. More books and three-ring binders were stacked on the floor under the small overhang where a guest's legs would go if they sat close to the desk, as if to examine or sign something. There are literally clear paths to walk, thought Chantal, who mentally summoned her mother in an effort to stop herself from getting up to explore the other room off Felicia's main office to satisfy her curiosity. Did the paths extend to other rooms which were hidden? How did Felicia move about? Where did these unseen rooms go? Did the rooms have rooms?

"So, anyway, I want to help. I'll do anything," Chantal swore, fervently having spelled out the reason she wrote a "cold-call" email asking for an audience.

"Oh," Felicia breathed, another one of her tells that she was excited, "Kip and I have stalled after our meeting with the other arts leaders in May. We spent most of April making an email list of arts leaders for the May meeting."

Felicia leaned in and smiled conspiratorially, "It was Kip who came up with the name we've kept, **KC MOlière: 400 in 2022**. We've been sending these flurries of emails as we try to figure out how to put on a festival of this size.

"He *delightfully* uses the Comic Sans MS font in *red*!" She giggled. "As opposed to my workmanlike black-ink prose. Like you, he is the idea person. What we need is someone with your energy and technological abilities to get us going again. We need to publish a newsletter to get the word out and to motivate the others to get moving on the project. Will you consider being the head of the Press and Publication Committee and write newsletters?"

Chantal fervently swore.

"*Mais, oui,*" Chantal immediately answered, thinking, I absolutely abhor doing newsletters. The formatting never comes out right...

It became evident, even four years before the birthday party and other cultural events, that the effort was already becoming unmanageable. A month later, Felicia hooked Becky Smith, author of the article that had prompted Chantal into action, as co-chair for the Press and Publication Committee.

The Rationale

 The 400th birthday of all-time greatest comic playwright Molière falls on Saturday, 15 January 2022.

 Kansas City's origins are French; it was settled by French fur-traders during Molière's lifetime.

 Kansas City is demonstrably one of the top cities in the USA for its embrace of the arts.

 Our troubled times cry out for a return to the classics and a focus on comedy (a genre that exposes universal human foibles).

The Vision

Every arts organization and every educational institution in the greater Kansas City area (including all of eastern Kansas and north central Missouri) will participate in **KC MOlière: 400 in 2022** by presenting theatre, dance, music, visual arts, puppets, films, lectures, workshops, or other events by or about Molière and/or his contemporaries, or work influenced by Molière's comic spirit, or new work translated/adapted from Molière's plays and comedy-ballets, or new work inspired by Molière's life and timeless themes.

Project Objectives

 To celebrate Molière, his work, and his theatrical and musical heritage

 To showcase Kansas City's special relationship with France and to encourage all forms of French-American cultural exchange

 To facilitate and coordinate Molière-related initiatives in all the arts and at all levels of education throughout greater Kansas City and the Missouri Valley region

 To enhance Kansas City's national and international visibility as a cosmopolitan city where the arts flourish

 To stimulate community spirit through the unifying power of laughter and enjoyment of universal foibles in the human condition

Allons, enfants!
Come Along, Children

Felicia was experiencing a *coup de foudre*. In other words, she was thunderstruck with love. Her Press and Publications Committee had moved the Molière festival along much faster than she and Kip in their nearly nine months of planning. Well, it wasn't really *her* Press and Publication Committee, but she was over the moon with Chantal's and Becky's progress.

Becky was perfect for the P&P Committee. She was the ideal foil to Chantal. Becky, with her dark hair and hazel eyes, was quiet until you got to know her, whereas Chantal was the archetypal redhead, with a fiery temper and lack of patience to boot.

Becky called to mind the ladies of the 1950s: gracious, inviting, well-mannered, and inquisitive. Chantal was a headstrong woman who preferred action to talk. Her father once told her that he liked giving her jobs to do because he knew they'd get done, while the other partners in his office would procrastinate. In her typical fashion, and focused on logic, Chantal thought this was a silly compliment. She was just doing her job.

Becky treated her admirers to her quick wit and charmed them with her humor. Chantal allowed hers to bow down in acquiescence. Becky was a natural-born journalist, capturing all the details of an event and subsequently bringing them to life with ink and paper. Chantal would fetch the ink and paper because Felicia had asked her to, and because Chantal liked Felicia.

Kip, as *de-facto* leader, regaled every potential collaborator with **KC MOlière: 400 in 2022**'s birth story as only an actor could do—capturing the imagination of those fortunate enough to hear him, spinning the narrative to make the audience forget where they were, and inspiring people to volunteer. He pitched opportunities to increase the public's awareness of the festival through similar projects such as the 200th Bicentennial of Missouri's statehood.

Unpublished article by Rebecca Smith

As we head toward our state's bicentennial in 2021, the celebration of KansasCity's French roots is picking up speed.

On March 6, City Hall hosted the unveiling of the first of four statues to be placed at the Chouteau Heritage Fountain in the Northland. The bronze statue, designed by local sculptor, Kwan Wu, honors the founder of Kansas City—fur trader, Francois Chouteau—as well as the Native Americans who lived and traded in the area.

The completed site will be comprised of the "river," represented by the fountain flowing over rocks, and three monumental statues perched on high, representing a trade exchange; fur trapping activity behind them will also be evident. The complex will accommodate groups and classes and will be illuminated at night. An ambitious project, it's not the only one to salute our "savoir faire."

Plans for **KC MOlière: 400 in 2022** are also proceeding steadily. The idea for the event—a six-month celebration of the playwright's birth in 1622—was introduced last spring.

Already available are the first two email newsletters (October 2018 and January 2019), as well as a Facebook page for Jean-Baptiste Poquelin (Molière's birth name) with more than 600 contacts to date. Watch as Kansas City's Gallic Flag begins to wave.

Ribbon cutting at Kansas City Hall with sculptor Kwan Wu
(Photo: Rebecca Smith)

Yet it was an uphill slog. Despite committees being formed, among them Fund-raising, Cultural, Music and Dance, and Visual and Popular Arts, Felicia despaired as the local press ignored news releases, such as Becky's combined report about the Chouteau Heritage Fountain and the festival's progress. Indeed, even once friendly art magazines bowed to internal politics and were unable to print submitted material. Many organizations and publication dismissed the Molière group by inviting it to submit its information to their website calendars, which merely listed all the "upcoming cultural events that readers might want to attend…"

Chantal was irritated with Kip. In reality, she was jealous of his sway over Felicia. It took her three weeks to figure out that the spelling of the event, KC MO*lière*, was a combination of KC (Kansas City) and MO (the postal abbreviation for Missouri). Such was the life of a newcomer to the city and its culture.

She resolved to explain, yet again, why **KC MOlière: 400 in 2022** needed a web presence in order to captivate the younger generations. It would just be *weird* if there weren't a website and some form of social media. The business would not look legitimate, at least in Chantal's humble opinion. Kip disagreed.

Kip and Chantal met for the first time in August 2018 at the Kansas City Actors Theatre showing of *Blithe Spirit*. After the play, Felicia, Kip, and Chantal, accompanied by their spouses, went to the restaurant at Union Station, an intoxicating hybrid of Gothic Revival and Second Empire architecture, which once saw 180 trains a day.

L to R: Felicia, Kip, and Chantal
(Photo: Venne Londré)

Pierpont's hadn't changed since its inception in 1914. It jealously guarded its three-story space with the women's smoking lounge, women's waiting room, and children's waiting room. What most awed Chantal was the fact she was floating in on Felicia's Backstage Clout to hang out with the actors after the show. Of course, the 20-foot bar with its own library ladder, impressed her spouse more and added to the ambiance of Really Cool After Party with Actors.

Felicia agreed with Kip's logic that it is better to talk with people than invite them to visit a website. Technology was a dreadfully tetchy thing that could decide it simply didn't wish to work any longer, and therefore all your work could simply poof! disappear.

She said, "I'm afraid a lot of people would not bother to seek out committees on a website. I think we have to keep the info here (1) because it's our greatest need after the newsletter and a full-time secretary or coordinator, and (2) because it shows that something thoughtful and serious came out of that May 21 meeting.

"If we can get some more chairpersons lined up, we could put a close-up photo of the individual chair next to their committee. That would both enliven the visual look of the newsletter, but most of all it would attract interest."

As September turned the leaves vibrant colors and the weather cooled, Becky and Chantal published the first newsletter, sending it to a group of 500 people in the Kansas City metropolitan area.

If I can't have a webpage, there are other ways to get to Gen X and Millennials, surmised Chantal. The Press and Publications Committee continued to move full-steam ahead under the close supervision of Chantal and Becky, who were precise in their coordination to keep the news and excitement about the festival ongoing via Molière's "personal" Facebook page.

The 397th birthday saw the publishing of the second newsletter to a growing number of devotees, and when the trees finally began to bud in the Spring of 2019—a full year after Kip had poked his head into Felicia's office—Chantal was attempting to explain to Phil, Becky's husband, who Molière was, exactly.

"Think of him like the French Shakespeare, except he didn't write tragedies."

"That is the way you should market him then. That is the way you will get people who don't know him to understand," Phil said. Of course, he was right, Becky thought. Americans knew Shakespeare, having studied him in high school. She had worked in advertising and knew how to get the message out to people. Her mind began to work on other press campaigns to entice the local media to favor the endeavor.

All of which came to a grinding halt when Chantal received a tearful call on May 6, 2019.

"Oh, Chantal," Felicia cried. "Kip has died."

Le valet est mort. Vive le valet!
The Valet Is Dead, Long Live the Valet!

The small group of Molière enthusiasts experienced the horror of time slowing down and the increased heart rate from adrenaline, similar to what happens when a driver slams on the brakes in the hopes of avoiding a rear-end collision caused by a sudden stop of traffic.

At the initial meeting in May 2018, Kip and Felicia had discussed the idea of obtaining a 501(c)(3) nonprofit status, but both had been reluctant to research this, as they hoped to become a pet project under the larger umbrella of KC Rep or KCAT, who not only had 501(c)(3)s, but also had more manpower and *savoir faire* when it came to launching a festival of this magnitude.

It was Kip who'd finagled donated goods, such as the French wine and cheese platters from Riemann's and Hy-Vee for that first meeting. It was he, acting as the faithful valet patiently guiding his master to the end result, who obtained audiences with Kansas City's intellectuals, like Megan Crigger, Consuelo Cruz, and Cheryl Kimmi, for advice on creating a fruitful festival.

Following Kip's death, Felicia felt overwhelmed to the point of drowning. It seemed her dream of celebrating Molière's 400th birthday was permanently gone, since the thought of picking up the fallen pieces to begin again left her bereft.

Kip Niven's Molière Legacy to Kansas City Lives On
By **Felicia Londré**
Spring/Summer 2019 Newsletter Vol. 2 No. 2

Kip Niven, the genius and motivator behind **KC MOlière: 400 in 2022**, passed away unexpectedly on 6 May. In the last 18 months of his life, he was devoted to preparing a world-class celebration of Molière's 400th birthday as a great gift to Kansas City.

Kip saw Molière's work as a prime source of joyful spirit that could bring together artists and audiences from all the visual, literary, and performing (theatre, music, dance, film, puppetry) arts to showcase our city's French heritage and the diversity of our contemporary cultural resources.

Kip Niven's leadership of KC MOlière: 400 in 2022 paralleled his shepherding of EARTh (Equity Actors Reading Theatre), which he founded with his friend **Doug Weaver**, who directed the company's readings of large-cast classic plays. In December 2017, they presented Molière's hilarious *The Doctor in Spite of Himself* (*Le Médecin malgré lui*).

Kip Niven
(Photo: Calan Welder)

Weaver recalls that talking about Molière with Kip had them giggling a lot. According to Weaver, "Kip loved the way an author who is often seen as highbrow could serve up the lowest of lowbrow humor and the way his comedies spawned so many varieties of theatre and dance, including farce, vaudeville, situation comedy...."

"Kip brought a boyish enthusiasm to the rehearsals," said **Martin Buchanan**, who played the bumptious title character Sganarelle in that EARTh performance. "It was infectious. If you didn't love Molière before, you would with this show." **Felicia Londré** saw the show and afterward enthused about it to Kip.

The Doctor in Spite of Himself must be signaled as the starting point for KC MOlière: 400 in 2022. Kip loved to tell "the origin story" to preface the interviews he and Felicia conducted as they sought advice on the project. Kip's partner and sweetheart, **Claudia Copping**, found that origin story in his own words among Kip's papers:

> *Some days later [after the December 2017 EARTh reading], I saw Felicia at UMKC and thanked her for her kind words. She said, "You know (I didn't) Molière's 400th birthday is coming up soon and I think we should do something to celebrate." I told her that if EARTh could help in any way, we would be glad to. Some weeks later I called her and suggested that we get together and discuss how to make this happen. The result is that we have formed a group of like-minded folks from across the KC Arts scene (Theatre, Opera, Ballet, The Nelson, The Symphony, etc.) to create a cross-city (indeed regional), cross-cultural celebration that will center on that 400th birthday (15 January 2022), but will have lead-up (sic) events (productions, lectures, workshops, etc.) throughout the 2021-'22 Theatre Season and academic school year. Our working title is…***KC MOlière: 400 in 2022.***

Kip's retelling is characteristically modest. He called and emailed Felicia in February and again in March before they finally met during her spring break.

A celebration of Kip Niven's remarkable life drew hundreds to the Kansas City Young Audiences event space on 26 May. The loving tributes culminated in a joyful sing-along of "Always Look on the Bright Side of Life" from *Monty Python's Life of Brian*. The upbeat spirit he promoted, even as we grieved our loss of Kip's physical presence, testifies to the importance of our carrying on with the Molière project to which he was committed.

Kip, *né* **Clifford Wallace Niven,** was born in Kansas City on 27 May 1945. He graduated from Shawnee Mission East High School and the University of Kansas. He was a Vietnam War veteran, serving three years in the United States Army. Some of Kip's career highlights include roles in movies like *Magnum Force* (1973) and Kevin Wilmott's *Jayhawkers* (2014); numerous television roles on shows including *The Waltons, Law and Order*, and three years (1982-5) on *Alice*; roles on Broadway in *Chess* (1988) and *Nick and Nora* (1991); and acting in radio and regional theatres, including Missouri Repertory Theatre/KC Rep.

In 1995, Kip moved back to Kansas City and conducted workshops, directed, served on boards, volunteered for arts organizations including KC Rep's educational programming, and represented Actors Equity Association.

Londré was excited to serve as co-convener with Kip on **KC MOlière: 400 in 2022**.

"We were finding our way together on how to put together a project of such scope," she says. "We would have flurries of exchanges of emails… Any quick glance at those emails will show that he was the idea person. Especially fun were our interviews with city leaders whose expertise we sought. And he would always begin those sessions with the origin story!"

Copping summarizes what Molière meant to Kip: "He appreciated the contemporary relevance and timelessness of Molière's work, and he thoroughly enjoyed the opportunity to work with Felicia. As ambitious and challenging in scope as the KC Molière project is, Kip's fearlessness and 'can do' attitude made him a positive force and a great collaborator."

It is heartening to know that everyone who worked with Kip is committed to seeing **KC MOlière: 400 in 2022** through to completion. We will be celebrating his memory along with that of his beloved Molière.

Prior to Kip's passing, he and Felicia met with an attorney who advised them to form a Limited Liability Company. Chantal had, a mere six months earlier, left the job which brought her to Kansas City and began her own company.

Chantal emailed Felicia. She registered the festival as an LLC with the State of Missouri and obtained a tax ID number. Like all the minor characters in Molière plays when their mistresses are stuck, she took control to engineer the outcome she wanted—but when the servants take control of the situation, the initial outcome often goes awry.

"I had to register my company, so I knew how to do it, and we don't need an attorney for that aspect. We will for a 501(c)(3). I don't know how to do that."

Buoyed by Chantal's action, Felicia reached out to her acquaintance, Don Dagenais, for further help. Don, with a warm eyes and a near constant smile, had been active for more than 40 years in in civic and community groups, particularly relating to the performing arts, and served on numerous boards of directors. A talented commercial real estate lawyer, he volunteered his time for the Kansas City

Volunteer Lawyers and Accountants for the Arts and the Volunteer Attorney Project, among others. He was the perfect choice to seek advice on the legalities and the next steps the festival needed to take if Felicia was to keep her dream alive.

He was a true gentleman who, upon seeing the havoc wreaked by the prior, incorrect advice, patiently gave step-by-step instructions to Felicia on undoing Chantal's enthusiastic, if misguided work. The LLC was dissolved and a new tax ID number obtained for the nonprofit corporation to be created. Felicia became the registered agent for the nonprofit corporation **KC MOlière: 400 in 2022**.

Don suggested a board of directors, naming Felicia and her two sup-

L to R: Becky Smith and Don Dagenais
(Photo: Felicia Londré)

porters, Chantal and Becky, as members. Bylaws were adopted, the Board was formed, and the process of legalizing **KC MOlière: 400 in 2022** began.

Nearly one month after Kip's passing, the **KC MOlière: 400 in 2022** Board of Directors met for the first time in a room off Felicia's office. Quick work was made to adopt the bylaws and begin the laborious process of obtaining a 501(c)(3), due to the unstinting help of Don with the required forms. **KC MOlière: 400 in 2022** would be the 25th arts organization in Kansas City that Don helped obtain a nonprofit status.

Meet Our Board Members!
Fall 2019 Newsletter, Vol. 2 No. 3

Your five-member Board of Directors had its initial meeting on 22 July. By-laws were adopted and officers were elected. The board voted to proceed with the incorporation and 501(c)(3) process; the application was mailed to the IRS on 24 July. Financial projections were discussed.

As president of the board, **FELICIA LONDRÉ** carries on the legacy of Kip Niven, founder of Equity Actors' Readers Theatre (EARTh), whose production of Molière's The Doctor in Spite of Himself on 4 December 2017 was the genesis of **KC MOlière: 400 in 2022**. Kip convinced Felicia to undertake what has become an increasingly large undertaking. Felicia is Curators' Distinguished Professor Emerita at UMKC where she is in her 42nd year of teaching theatre history. She earned her BA in French at the University of Montana, her MA in Romance Languages at the University of Washington, Seattle, and her Ph.D. in Speech/Theatre at the University of Wisconsin-Madison, where she directed plays in French and English. She was pleased to get two minutes at the inaugural gathering of the Theatre Alliance of Kansas City (TAKC) on 12 August to tell about **KC MOlière: 400 in 2022**, Inc.

SARAH INGRAM-EISER joined the board as vice president, having offered her assistance in arts endeavors when she and Felicia Londré sat together in the audience of a Black Repertory Theatre of KC production. Sarah graduated from Scripps College in California where she began lifelong friendships with leaders in the arts. She served as chair of the original Missouri Repertory Theatre (now KC Rep) Guild as well as numerous other community and arts boards. Sarah brings her experience as a tax associate for H&R BLOCK and as an international theatregoer ever since her year of study at the University of Florence.

JIM WEITZEL, board treasurer, has opened a bank account for KC MOlière: 400 in 2022, Inc. and is working with Fundraising co-chairs **Don Dagenais** and **Bev Elving**. Jim brings to the board his experience from a career in commercial real estate marketing and development. He earned his B.S. in Economics at Wharton School of the University of Pennsylvania and an MBA in Marketing from the University of Michigan Business School. Jim has served on the boards of the Folly Theatre (board president 2011-12), the Unicorn, the American Jazz Museum, and the Homeowners Association of Kansas City. Jim and his wife, **Sarah Minogue Weitzel**, are also strong supporters of KC Melting Pot Theatre.

Secretary of the board, **CHANTAL ROBERTS**, has contributed far beyond her secretarial duties. As co-chair of the Press and Publications Committee, she has edited every issue of the newsletter, created our website and maintained a 'personal' Facebook page for Jean-Baptiste Poquelin. She answers myriad emails in the persona of Molière's secretary, so it's not surprising that she loves to wear costumes and looks forward to a masquerade-ball 399th birthday gala on 15 January 2021. Chantal graduated from Baylor University with dual majors in French and Radio-TV-Film. She and her husband, **Aaron Roberts**, moved from Little Rock, Arkansas, to Overland Park in July 2018, just in time to see **Rebecca Smith**'s article on the Molière project in *KC Studio magazine*.

With moving crates not yet unpacked, Chantal tracked down Felicia Londré and signed on initially to help with the newsletter, but Chan**tal** has a way of taking initiative, even as she runs her own business, CMR Consulting.

After **KC MOlière: 400 in 2022**'s founder **Kip Niven** passed away, Press & Publication co-chairs, Chantal Roberts and **REBECCA (Becky) SMITH**, became the main rallying forces to keep our efforts going. Becky grew up in the St. Louis area and graduated from Indiana University with studies at the University of Hamburg, Germany. Becky and her husband, **Phil Smith**, met in Chicago, where they both worked in advertising. They and their three children have lived in New Zealand, Australia, Thailand, and Ann Arbor. Becky is an avid supporter of the arts in Kansas City, as you can tell from her articles in *KC Studio* magazine.

All five board members are active contributors to the work of our committees. The Board of Directors especially looks forward to hiring an administrative assistant who can…oversee the board's growing list of initiatives.

Chantal was exceedingly pleased with herself since she nabbed the domain kcmoliere400in2022.com on June 11, 2019 and created a website for the festival. The Press and Publication Committee chose Catherine Rush Thompson to be the Blogger-in-Chief so that the public, and later the media, would have information about the ties between this unknown (at least in the United States) playwright and the Heartland. Felicia wrote the first blog, "My Favorite Exploration of Molière's Comedic Genius," on June 18, 2019, although she quibbled about the use of the word "favorite." She mused, "At least the book has a fresh, general appeal."

Committees were established with co-chairs who would best shepherd their volunteers into recognizing the Board's—really Felicia's—vision.

COMMITTEE	CO-CHAIRS
College & University Education	**Jennifer Martin & Mechele Leon**
Commercial	TBD
Cultural Context	**Linda Ade Brand & Tracy Terstriep Herber**
Financial	**Don Dagenais**
Fundraising	**Bev Elving**
International Relations	**Cyprienne Simchowitz**
K-12 Education	**Martin English & Doug Weaver**
Logistics and Governing	TBD
Social Planning	**Claire Davis**
Theatrical Production	**John Rensenhouse & Sidonie Garret**
Thoroughly Modern Molière	**Cynthia Levin & Damron Russel Armstrong**
15 January 2022 Gala	TBD

Continuing to move at lightning speed for a volunteer organization, on July 22, 2019, the Board signed the Articles of Incorporation and the bylaws. Don was the first signatory on July 17, 2019. After all that, Don agreed to serve as co-chair of the Financial and Fundraising Committee.

Felicia had survived the death of the co-convener, and now dreamed of French Baroque concerts, art exhibits, and theatre productions with an evening gala benefit masked ball at the Nelson-Atkins Rozelle Court after a free-to-the-public birthday party with four 100-candles to celebrate its success.

It was a sign of her naïveté, Felicia would later recollect, that she still believed she could easily win over the American public with Molière and have 8,000 people attend his birthday party.

College & University Education Committee

To encourage study of Molière and his era as well as production of his plays and/or spinoffs of his plays. Suggested membership: Representatives from each KC area institution of higher learning.

Cultural Context Committee

To encourage and coordinate activities in music, dance, painting, and other arts related to Molière and 17th-century Baroque and/or neoclassical culture. ***Suggested membership:*** Representatives from each art museum, musical group, dance company, puppet company, etc.

29

Fundraising Committee

To raise funds to support the coordinating initiatives and other costs not borne by the producing organizations. May create a separate committee to oversee financials. ***Suggested membership:*** Experienced fundraisers and gala organizers.

International Relations Committee

To seek opportunities for participation in the Kansas City 2021-22 season of Molière by artists and organizations from France. ***Suggested membership:*** French-speaking and/or world-traveling volunteers.

K-12 Education Committee

To generate curriculum and programming in the schools with activities that might include workshops, performances, French-language events, field trips, study guides. ***Suggested membership:*** K-12 educators.

Press and Publications Committee

To handle the social media pages (Facebook, Twitter, Instagram) and to oversee printed materials: brochures, news stories, media outlets, and the 2022 collectible souvenir booklet. ***Suggested membership:*** Writers, editors, social media savvy and witty persons.

Theatrical Production Committee

To coordinate play selections and scheduling of stage productions for the celebration period. ***Suggested membership:*** Representatives from each professional theatre producing group.

Thoroughly Modern Molière Committee

To encourage new plays about the life of Molière or inspired by his comic spirit or in the form of adaptations of his work to feature diverse contemporary cultures, and to facilitate the production of such new work during the 2021-22 season as part of Kansas City's internationally visible **KC MOlière: 400 in 2022**. ***Suggested membership:*** Theatre artists of color, dramaturgs.

Mon Cœur
My Love

August 2019 proved to be a productive month for Felicia.

Journalists generally prefer to remain in the background so they can more easily observe life, but Becky was the dynamism behind the "getting to know you" party on August 6, 2019, to gauge the commitment level of the volunteers and energize them for the long road ahead.

"Every place is expensive," Felicia complained.

"We should also consider parking and mobility issues," continued Becky.

Chantal, throwing a wrench into the planning, suggested, "It doesn't matter for me, since I work for myself and from home, but if we're looking for volunteers, we can't really start the party at 4 p.m. because people are still working. I mean, maybe they can get off early at 4:30, but I'd start the party at 5 at the earliest."

Chantal, who was getting to know her new friends, could see the wheels turning in Becky's mind when her eyes lit up, "The Diastole Scholars Center… what about that?"

"I don't know what that is," Chantal said, hating her status as so new to the city since it made her feel useless for the most part.

Felicia again attempted to contain her excitement and energy. "The Center is an exquisitely beautiful home built in 1976 by Dr. E. Grey Dimond, the founder of UMKC's School of Medicine! It's named after the stage when the heart relaxes and a person's blood pressure decreases."

The space fit the fledgling organization's needs perfectly since it was an appealing area offered to organizations on the periphery who had smaller monetary resources.

Felicia couldn't relax just yet into her position—everything was still so new and confusing—but at the party Becky organized, complete with donated French wines à la their first meeting, she felt closer to Molière and her dream than ever before.

Becky and Felicia firmed up the agenda, allowing everyone to tour the house with its large, circular beige couch in the piano room, aptly named for the grand concert Steinway which was coveted by the UMKC Conservatory for recitals.

L to R: Dawn Youngs, Fred Homan, Cynthia Levin, and Lindsay Adams Kennedy
(Photo: Felicia Londré)

Separated by a wall, the sunroom sported beer steins and a bar space where early volunteers poured generous glasses of the aforementioned donated wine. But what made Becky suggest the Diastole, and made Felicia agree, was the kiva.

The kiva, a traditional meeting space of the indigenous Pueblo people, was an amphitheater-like room. The co-chairs gave brief talks about their committees in the kiva, hoping to entice more people to share the work and reduce the burden of what needed to be done.

A theme seemed to emerge over the course of the evening:

 To celebrate Molière, his work, and his theatrical and musical heritage

 To showcase Kansas City's special relationship with France and to encourage all forms of French-American cultural exchange

 To facilitate and coordinate Molière-related initiatives in all the arts and at all levels of education throughout greater Kansas City and the Missouri Valley region

Cynthia Levin, from the Unicorn Theatre, and Damron Russel Armstrong, with the Black Repertory Theatre of Kansas City, co-chairs of the Thoroughly Modern Molière committee, received a jumpstart.

"We're are commissioning a new play influenced by the life of Molière…," Cynthia said.

"…Or inspired by his comic spirit…," Damron continued.

"Yes! Or in the form of adaptations, alterations, of his work featuring a diverse cast," Cynthia continued. "The proposal deadline is January 1, 2020."

The volunteers murmured amongst themselves in hushed tones about the fact that the due date was a mere five months away.

Midway through the committee presentations, the gathering was treated to three Baroque period performances. Claire Davis (Co-Chair of the Social Committee with Georgianna Buchanan) performed a soliloquy from Tartuffe, *en français*, which became the inspiration for the 398th and 399th birthday party events; Tracy Terstriep Herber, with the lithe, graceful, and unselfconscious movements that only someone who has not only lived and breathed dance, but also sweated and bled it, demonstrated how the courtiers basking in Louis XIV's sunrays would promenade (almost as if dancing) about the gardens of Versailles.

"In fact, when courtiers stopped walking," Tracy also stopped, pointing to her feet, "they were in the third ballet position, with the right foot at an angle while the left foot's arch was near the heel of the outturned right foot."

While teaching court ballet deportment, Tracy was ably accompanied by cellist, Trilla Ray-Carter. The final intermission's entertainment was Ryan Head, UMKC graduate student in guitar studies, who performed a piece by Molière's contemporary, Robert de Visée. Ryan later commented, "I wasn't sure what to expect, and to be honest, I had imagined something rather stuffy and academic. I couldn't have been more wrong! Everyone was so charming and enthusiastic; I was filled with optimism for your project."

Ryan Head
(Photo: Felicia Londré)

Claire Davis
(Photo: Felicia Londré)

Rounding out the committee updates, Jennifer Martin and Mechele Leon, co-chairs of the Higher Education Committee, also had jump-started their subsection of the organization by calling a meeting for September 20, 2019. They were excited and ready to get started, knowing that universities and colleges needed plenty of lead time to get through the academic and bureaucratic quagmire. Stephanie Roberts, Co-Chair of *UMKC Theatre's Molière* initiatives, highlighted her idea for a Mobile Molière project, which would end up being instrumental in introducing this Frenchman to a new, never-before-reached audience.

L to R Front: Volunteer, Dani Trebus, and Collin Vorbeck
(Photo: Felicia Londré)

Not to be outdone by tertiary education, Martin English and Dani Trebus, co-chairs for K-12 Education, were feverishly preparing for the upcoming school year which was scheduled to start in mere weeks, and they also had already begun reaching out to area schools to promote Molière and French studies.

"I am thrilled to report the support of Jeff Church and The Coterie Theatre, one of Kansas City's children theatre groups," Martin proudly declared. Martin, executive director of Kansas City Young Audiences, which strove to provide schools with professional teaching artists, classroom workshops, and arts-in-education programs, was a perfect leader for this committee.

He was evenly matched with Dani, whose theatre career in education and performance spanned 30 years. As the theatre teacher at Staley High School in North Kansas City, she was well familiar with secondary education.

"And once we finish writing them, we will distribute our programs and educational guides on the website. These will break down everything a teacher needs to know about Molière, complete with questions, answers, and tangential information—anything a teacher could want to make a test for, or give as a handout before the students see the play…" Dani's voice trailed off, thinking, making sure she had hit all the information she and Martin had agreed on. She decided she had given all the information and smiled at the volunteers.

Felicia was particularly anxious to have the educational committees start early, since they would lead everyone into the year-long **KC MOlière: 400 in 2022** festival. The school year started in August; doing the math, then, the festival would start with the school plays in August and September 2021, or in exactly two years.

When Felicia thought about all the moving parts, it made her chest so tight that she couldn't breathe. The amount of work was insurmountable—but this group! Becky, Chantal, Cynthia, Mechele, Tracy, Martin, all the committee cochairs kept pushing, and slowly they moved off center from Kip's sudden and tragic death.

Cyprienne Simchowitz, chair of the International Committee, had been quietly working away with her contacts in France, letting them know about the organization and festival. She shattered the trope that blondes don't have brains, for she studied international law and economics at the University of Paris, and obtained her juris doctor from the University of Missouri-Kansas City School of Law. She practiced law in both France and the States. She was also impossibly *chic* the way only the French can be.

The presentation had been an entire hour of entertainment in the kiva, including the cochairs' pleas for volunteers to sign up for their committees. Most of them were accustomed to winning over audiences regularly, and they did exactly that.

INTERNATIONAL EYES ON KANSAS CITY IN JANUARY 2022
French Comic Playwright's 400th Birthday
Inspires Metro-wide Celebration

KANSAS CITY, Mo. – Kansas City's national reputation as a major theatre city is poised for international recognition with anticipated French media coverage of the biggest birthday celebration outside of France for 17th century comic dramatist Molière. A free-to-the-public party with a 400-candle cake will happen on January 15, 2022. It's one event in a nine-month season of festivities.

The party will be the centerpiece of multiple events coordinated and supported by KC MOlière: 400 in 2022, Inc., a 501(c)(3) nonprofit organization, spearheaded by the late actor **Kip Niven** and **Felicia Hardison Londré**, Curators' Distinguished Professor Emerita of Theatre at UMKC.

Arts and education events are already in the works, beginning in September 2021 and continuing throughout the 2021/22 arts season. Theatres committed to including a Molière play or adaptation or work inspired by his comic spirit include **Kansas City Actors Theatre**, the **Unicorn Theatre, Black Repertory Theatre of Kansas City**, and **The Coterie. UMKC Theatre** plans a Mobile Molière touring unit to perform a Molière one-act in middle schools. **Kansas City Baroque Consortium** and **Owen Cox Dance Group** are among the music and dance groups that will participate.

"There are so many cultural tie-ins with the Metro area," said Londré, president of **KC MOlière: 400 in 2022**, Inc. "We have Kansas City's French founders settling here in 1822, exactly midway between Molière's birthdate of January 15, 1622, and our 2021-22 festivities."

Cyprienne Simchowitz, Chair of the International Committee and Honorary Consul of the French Republic for Kansas and Western Missouri, attended the Volunteer Kickoff for **KC MOlière: 400 in 2022**. Simchowitz stated that her French contacts will assist in obtaining French cooperation and coverage for the **KC MOlière: 400 in 2022** events. The Volunteer Kickoff was August 6, 2019, at the Diastole Scholars' Center in Kansas City, Mo.

Simchowitz reiterated one of **KC MOlière: 400 in 2022**'s stated goals: to turn a national and international spotlight on Kansas City's thriving arts community and arts audiences.

Molière has been translated into every major language and remains one of the most-produced playwrights in the world. His comedies form the core repertoire of the famed *Comédie Française* in Paris. The social foibles and pretensions he plays upon with warm humor and sharp wit are timeless.

Tartuffe especially has had some politically charged interpretations over the years. Having twice played that title character, **John Rensenhouse**, managing director of **KC Actors Theatre**, knows firsthand the range of comic possibilities. He used a choice tidbit from *Tartuffe* to introduce his Theatrical Production Committee at the recent Volunteer Kickoff party. His committee, co-chaired by **Heart of America Shakespeare Festival** director **Sidonie Garrett**, is charged with overseeing participation by Kansas City's professional theatre companies.

About 60 people attended the Volunteer Kickoff where chairs of seven committees described their missions. Entertainment included Broadway dancer **Tracy Terstriep**'s demonstration of Baroque court ballet postures and steps. Guitarist **Ryan Head** played selections by Molière's contemporary, Robert de Visée. **Claire Davis** performed a Molière monologue in French.

"I was surprised to learn that well over half of Molière's work was music-based," said Londré. "His court ballets were created in collaboration with composers like Lully and Charpentier. Their work, along with Baroque painting and garden landscaping and other arts, made the Sun King's reign one of the most vibrant in western history."

L to R: Dan Klinger and Mechele Leon
(Photo: Felicia Londré)

An educational goal of **KC MOlière: 400 in 2022** is to reach students of all ages from kindergarten to higher education and instill enjoyment of the classics as a foundation for appreciation of contemporary arts. **Martin English**, Executive Director of **Kansas City Young Audiences**, and **Dani Trebus**, Director of Theatre at Staley High School, co-chair the K-12 Committee, of which the **Académie Lafayette** is a key player. Twenty-seven area colleges and universities have representatives on the Higher Education Committee headed by **Jennifer Martin**, UMKC Hall Family Foundation Professor Emerita, and **Mechele Leon**, University of Kansas Associate Professor of Theatre.

KC MOlière: 400 in 2022 is a festival that will run from September 2021 through 2022 in the greater Kansas City Metro area, featuring theatre, film, dance, music, visual arts, puppetry, book clubs, food, and wine. Venues, times, and dates TBA.

For access to the four newsletters published to date, visit the website, KCMoliere400in2022.com.

KC MOlière: 400 in 2022 is a community organization that seeks to celebrate Molière, his work, and his theatrical and musical heritage while showcasing Kansas City's special relationship with France, thereby enhancing Kansas City's national and international visibility as a cosmopolitan city where the arts flourish.

KC MOlière: 400 in 2022 Volunteer Kickoff
August 6, 2019, at the Diastole, Kansas City, Mo.

L to R: Damron Russel Armstrong, Executive Artistic Director of the Black Repertory Theatre of Kansas City and Cynthia Levin, Producing Artistic Director of the Unicorn Theatre.

Cyprienne Simchowitz, Honorary Consul of the French Republic (foreground right), addresses the audience. Sitting are KC MOlière: 400 in 2022 Board Members Rebecca Smith (front row left) and Chantal Roberts (front row right)

KC MOlière: 400 in 2022 Volunteer Kickoff
August 6, 2019, at the Diastole, Kansas City, Mo.

Audience including from center to right,
UMKC Instructor Venne Londré (front row
center), and UMKC Associate Professor
of Physical Theatre, Stephanie Roberts
(front row right)

Tracy Terstriep, Director of Theatre,
Upper School Performing Arts Chair at
Pembroke Hill School, performing 17th c.
French dance

A week later, Jim and Felicia had the **KC MOlière: 400 in 2022** bank account set up.

Felicia went to the post office to check the mail three days before the start of the school year, on August 23, 2019. She always liked the post office. It smelled like cardboard boxes and paper; that smell meant a package or a letter was on its way somewhere, possibly far away—or perhaps, a box had just arrived from a far-flung, never-before-heard-of island. The possibilities were endless and intoxicating to think about.

Her slender hand pulled an envelope from the PO Box and halted. To say Felicia's heart sank or she girded her loins would be trite metaphors. Instead, it was more like she anticipated bad news. In a country where Shakespeare was studied and classic theatre mostly treated as the unwanted and unloved stepchild, the high of the volunteer party three weeks earlier had waned as she worked on interviewing to hire an administrative assistant.

The search for the assistant was tedious, as she had never before hired someone for this type of work. Felicia supposed it was a benefit of having lived in academia for her entire life. If an assistant was needed—and approved—the university's hiring personnel would do the vetting.

Don assured Felicia that the assistant could write all necessary letters and grant applications, perform marketing duties, take minutes at the board meetings, coordinate contracts for venues, photographers, musicians, actors, hotels, printers and volunteers, and update the website and newsletters for $450 a month. Yet she dared not hope. Jim stated they did not yet have the money to support an administrative assistant, even on a part-time basis, and it seemed that Fate had cut the thread of this dream.

So, she sat in her car, looking at the impossibly official—and somewhat intimidating-looking—envelope from the Internal Revenue Service. This would be the news that they did not have the coveted tax-exempt status so needed to encourage donors to part with their money.

Felicia recalled that stress invaded every fiber of her body the day she completed the application. She had set aside a two-hour block of uninterrupted time, and meticulously and precisely, as if she were creating a work of art, Felicia labored. She even handwrote the application code number at the top of the application, which numbered more than 40 pages. Then she wrote the check for $600, never claiming any reimbursement, as she rushed to the Westport post office with just minutes to spare before its 5 p.m. closing. She sent the application via overnight express with a hope and a prayer to Molière that her diligence would impress the IRS regarding the festival's significance.

She tore the envelope, unfolded the letter, and reading the first sentence was very happy she'd had the wherewithal to open the letter in the car where she was seated.

```
Dear Applicant:

We're pleased to tell you we determined you're exempt from federal income tax
under Internal Revenue Code (IRC) Section 501(c)(3). Donors can deduct
contributions they make to you under IRC Section 170. You're also qualified
to receive tax deductible bequests, devises, transfers or gifts under
Section 2055, 2106, or 2522. This letter could help resolve questions on your
exempt status. Please keep it for your records.
```

"Someone in the IRS must like Molière!" Felicia giddily informed the Board. "Don said it easily takes 3-6 months, but five weeks after I submitted the 40-page application, we received notification that we have our 501(c)(3)!"

Becky imagined Felicia typing this breathlessly while simultaneously attempting to sit still, but failing to do so. She smiled because she could also hear (in her head) Felicia muttering under her breath as she struggled with her outdated computer which routinely attempted to subvert her. While there are benefits of living in academia, there are also problems, such as a labyrinthian IT department and the accomplishment of Herculean feats to prove oneself worthy of a new computer.

What consumed Felicia's attention now was ordering letterhead with the forthcoming logo and preparing said letterhead for Board signatures to send to donors, prodding all committees and arts organizations, and beginning a master calendar of productions with possible dates. In short, herding a dozen theatre companies full of *artistes* to plan more than three months ahead while simultaneously overseeing the co-chairs and their 40 volunteers.

Felicia emailed herself and copied the board about a possible administrative assistant candidate and called for a Board Meeting on October 8. She wondered if the ability to read and converse in French would be a plus—knowing how she wanted to attract the *Comédie Française* and other French dignitaries to the celebration. However, the group currently had a $600 balance in its account, with projected expenditures of $20,000.

"My dad always said you have to spend money to make money," Chantal consoled Felicia. Not that this was much consolation, since they couldn't pay an admin assistant to begin organizing the fundraising necessities such as letterhead, compiling mailing lists, chasing theatres... Felicia wondered again which came first.

"But fun fact: you don't have to order letterhead on paper any longer. You can set it as a header and slap it on the Word document when it gets printed. And if you need to change something, like a phone number, you do it right away without having all this wasted stock you can no longer use because it has the wrong number on it. And it's free."

Felicia was fluent in French, but she had not one iota of an idea what Chantal had just said.

Don, who was not yet on the Board, emailed saying he'd run into their first choice at another board meeting where she served as its administrative assistant. She told him that she was quite interested in the Molière job and, in fact, had been reading up on Molière! As any administrative assistant worth their salt, she didn't bat an eye when she heard the Board needed help with grant writing. She merely smiled and said, "That is what I do for a living."

By September 27, 2019, **KC MOlière: 400 in 2022** had an administrative assistant to handle technical matters (like the long process of adding the photos back into the newsletter on the newly redesigned website), grant-writing, timeline oversight, trips to the printer, and dozens of additional tasks that would have been overlooked if left to **KC MOlière: 400 in 2022**'s volunteer leadership.

Les Obstacles
Obstacles

*C*hantal was excited there was to be an administrative assistant because she hoped to foist the newsletter onto this unsuspecting newbie. While she was on the Board, she had this overwhelming fear of missing out because she was not invited by all the cool kids; so she deployed her time-honored tradition of buttering up the administrative assistants.

It's a well-known fact, Chantal pontificated to herself, that you don't befriend the boss. They're used to people kissing up to them. Nope. Become friends with the people who know where the paperclip stash is kept and the bodies are buried. *That's* how you get ahead in the world.

Chantal hoped the September 2019 newsletter would be her last. She'd already succeeded in dropping the website into the admin's lap, and she had adroitly brought the assistant up to speed, and suggested, due to continuing technical issues, that Felicia be emailed at the beginning and end of the week with a "to-do" and a "was-done" list. This worked well, allowing Felicia to check off the list of chores from the analog master list.

Kansas City, the City of Fountains, was preparing a ribbon cutting for a new fountain and art installation on Choteau Trafficway. The fountain promised to honor the past, showing the river bluffs where Rock Creek and the Missouri River converge, located mere blocks from the site of François Chouteau's original fur trading post, with three statues depicting trading between the Indigenous People and the Europeans while in another area a Native American trapper hunts his prey.

The problem was the city was having a press conference at a strip of land with no address, and Chantal, still being new to the city, got lost several times in her attempt to attend the dedication on Tuesday, November 15, 2019, for social media photos. It was still a burden to get people engaged in **KC MOlière: 400 in 2022**, despite creating Twitter and Instagram accounts for the festival, both of which the administrative assistant handled, thank goodness.

Rushing in 10 minutes late, just as the speeches began, and sliding into a seat next to Felicia, Chantal breathed deeply and enjoyed the fact that even though the air was the type of cold that hurt your lungs, the sun was strong enough to give you a sunburn in an hour. She hoped to take some photos and get back to work. She hated these kinds of events, with everyone talking about how important they were and attempting to one up each other. Chantal didn't even like attending these kinds of ceremonies when she was one of the honorees.

Pictured: (at the podium) Keith Nelson. Seated behind are (second row) Kwan Wu, the sculptor of the sculpture group that would include François Chouteau and Osage and Kansa natives, and (front row) Vann Bighorse, who gave the blessing of the ground in the Osage language. (Photo: Felicia Londré)

Felicia suggested a partnership at the inauguration of the François Chouteau & Native American Heritage Fountain with the Chouteau Fountain founders, co-chaired by Keith Nelson. She wanted to promote joint activities to tie Molière's birthday celebrations to the summer 2021 bicentennial of François Chouteau's founding of Kansas City in cooperation with the Osage and Kansa people.

In addition to the collaboration with the State of Missouri adding traction to the organization, International Liaison Cyprienne Simchowitz and her co-chair, Dorothée Werner, shared the wonderful news that they had convinced Dr. Virginie Roche-Tiengo, a professor at the Sorbonne, to spend a week in Kansas City in spring 2020. This not only meant international eyes on Kansas City, but also a slow warmup to the big birthday festival in 2022, giving local media time to catch up and learn about their mission.

Felicia Londré pictured with local student portraying François Chouteau
(Photo: Chantal Roberts)

Dr. Roche-Tiengo, who teaches legal English at the Université de Paris where she is the assistant dean for international and institutional relations and speaks with a soft, lilting Irish accent, delivered an even bigger coup to the Board: she had spoken with Jérôme Pouly, a *sociétaire de la Comédie Française* (an actor who is a "partner member" of the illustrious theatre company founded in the 17th century). Jérôme was extremely interested in the project and invited Dr. Roche-Tiengo and Cyprienne to meet with him at the *Comédie Française* so he could share his ideas for the festival.

The Cultural Context Committee had so many ideas that it split and formed two committees, which promised to fulfill Felicia's original vision for the festival. Linda Ade Brand and Tracy Terstriep Herber continued to oversee the Cultural Context while they simultaneously co-chaired the Music and Dance Committee. They also met with Nelson-Atkins Education Director, Adam Johnson, and Adult Program Director, Cat Mueller, to discuss potential collaborations with the museum. Trudie Homan and Beth Byrd-Lonski graciously acquiesced to co-chair the Visual and Popular Arts Committee that included areas such as puppetry, pantomime, film, libraries, and book clubs, demonstrating a foresight none of the Board had seen as important in late 2019.

The organization had been limping along with an amateurish logo hurriedly designed by Chantal, comprised of the fleur-de-lis.

The Board of **KC MOlière: 400 in 2022** commissioned local artist Christina Schafer, who generously donated her time and talent to create a new logo. With Kansas City in the foreground of the French fleur-de-lis flag, it was a direct nod to Kansas City's French past and its link to Molière. Felicia later said, "Christina really came through for us by tying together today's Kansas City and a lovely evocation of 17th century France." Never one to miss an opportunity for self-promotion, the Press and Publication committee asked fans to weigh in on social media, using the hashtag #KCMOlierenewlogo.

As the weather continued to cool, the Board began to look toward celebrating Molière's 398th birthday, suggesting places such as a private home or perhaps a theatre while it was "dark," meaning it had no show in production at the time. But as the birthday approached, other problems began to present themselves.

The amount of work being done by the volunteers, or rather, the lack of work, was making Felicia anxious. It would take time and money to get things up and running, neither of which the organization had much of due to people still not knowing who Molière was, and his birthday *fête* a mere two years away. Some committees were not carrying their weight—indeed not even doing their job—thrusting their work onto the already-overloaded assistant.

"When Kip Niven and I got together on March 28, 2018, to chat about what might be done to celebrate the 400th birthday of Molière," Felicia said, "we naively thought we would not need funding or a formal organization because all our city's theatre companies would just naturally do their share as part of what they do. How wrong we were about funding and everyone doing their part!

"We didn't foresee that things like marketing and educational outreach need upfront funding," Felicia admitted.

Kansas City Royalty Celebrates Molière on His 398th Birthday
by **Rebecca Smith**
Spring 2020 Newsletter Vol. 3 No. 1

Over his career, Molière often played to royalty. In a turnabout, to celebrate his 398th birthday on Jan 15, 2020, Kansas City royalty played Molière.

The memorable evening began just after 5 at Just Off-Broadway Theatre (generously hosted by **Linda** and **Harvey Williams**). For roughly forty minutes, guests nibbled on canapés, quaffed French wines, socialized and were charmed by the flowing harp melodies of **Calvin Arsenia**.

Then all guests filed into the theatre space (coming close to filling it) and prepared to be enveloped in Molière's wit and wisdom.

A swath of Kansas City celebrities paired off for readings of Molière excerpts. Most extracts were humorous, some were poignant, one was disturbing. It was clear that all in attendance were highly entertained—the performers as much as the audience.

Calvin Arsenia
(Photo: Felicia Londré)

The glittering Court of Molière included:

- **Charles Bruffy**
  Artistic Director of KC Chorale

- **Tyrone Aiken**
  Artistic Director of KC Friends of Alvin Ailey

- **Andrea Tudhope**
  Award-winning Reporter at
  KCUR

- **Rashida Phillips**
  New Executive Director of the
  American Jazz Museum

- **Consuelo Cruz**
  Arts Marketing Coordinator,
  Office of Culture and Creative
  Services

- **Calvin Arsenia**
  Harpist/Singer/Songwriter/Poet
  Extraordinaire

- **René Bollier**
  President/Owner of Andre's
  Confisserie Suisse

- **Stuart Carden**
  New Artistic Director, KC Rep

- **Zach Moores**
  Entrepreneur/Owner of Crow's Coffee

- **Cynthia Levin**
  Artistic Director, Unicorn Theatre

- **Heidi Van**
  Actor/Creator/Director, Black Box Theatre

- **Peregrine Honig**
  Artist/Owner of Birdie's/Artistic Director, 18th St. Fashion Show

- **Nicole Hodges Persley**
  Associate Director of Theatre, UMKC

- **Cyprienne Simchowitz**
  International Attorney/Recent Honorary French Consul

- **Sean O'Harrow**
  Executive Director, Kemper Museum

- **Christopher Leitch**
  Visual Artist/Educator/Nature Lover

L to R: Ron Megee as CLIMENE and
Victoria Botero as URANIE, reading from
Tim Mooney's translation of *The Critique
of the School for Wives*
(Photo: Felicia Londré)

- **Whitney Terrell**
  Author/Professor at UMKC

- **Ron Megee**
  Actor/Director, Late Night Theatre

- **Victoria Sofia Botero**
  Soprano/Producer/Historian

Readings (ranging far beyond the familiar *Tartuffe*) included:

- *Lover's Quarrels*

- *Two Precious Maidens Ridiculed*

- *The Doctor in Spite of Himself*

- *The Would-Be Gentleman*

- David Ives's *The School for Lies*, an adaptation of *The Misanthrope*

- Christopher Hampton's *The Philanthropist* (a mirror opposite to *The Misanthrope*)

- Mikhail Bulgakov's *Molière or the Cabal of Hypocrites*

- *The Miser*

- *The Critique of the School of Wives*

Non-reading dignitaries glittered, as well. Molière's words rang out to:

- **Keith Nelson**
  Co-Chair of the Chouteau Fountain Founders, highlighting Kansas City's French origins

- **Carrie Coogan**
  New Acting Director of KC Public Libraries

- **Megan Crigger**
  Director of Creative Services, Office of Culture and Creative Services

- **Cheryl Kimmi**
  Executive Director, KC Fringe Festival and KC Creates

- **Christina Schafer**
  Workflow Manager, Garmin International

- **Col. William Eckhardt**
  Professor Emeritus, UMKC School of Law; Chief Prosecutor for My Lai Trials

- **Stuart Hinds**
  Assistant Dean of LaBudde Special Collections, Miller Nichols Library and Founder/Curator of Gay and Lesbian Archives of Mid-America

Far from merely attending, many have been instrumental in promoting **KC MOlière: 400 in 2022**. **Megan Crigger** and **Cheryl Kimmi** were among the first people interviewed by **Felicia Londré** and **Kip Niven** about the prospective city-wide 400th birthday celebration. **Christina Schafer** designed the striking logo. **Linda** and **Harvey Williams** coordinated the theater space, even disrupting their rehearsal commitments.

Sending their regrets but indicating interest, **Mayor Quinton Lucas** and **Julián Zugazagoitia** will surely join us at future events.

Felicia Londré, Curators' Distinguished Professor Emerita of Theatre and President of **KC MOlière: 400 in 2022**, Inc., acted as Hostess/Grande Dame of the evening, flamboyantly introducing, instructing and generally captivating ev

L to R: Chantal Roberts and Felicia Londré
(Photo: Venne Londré)

eryone on and off the stage. Not to mention stepping in effortlessly to perform, when a scheduled reader couldn't make it.

Also working diligently to support the event were the **KC MOlière: 400 in 2022**, Inc. Board and Committees. Warranting special recognition were **Fred Homan** for his gallant bartending, **Marshall** and **Mary Rimann** for the generously discounted fine wine, **Patricia Williams** at the nametag table, and **Georgianna Buchanan** for coordinating the Geaux Catering table of appetizers.

Reactions were roundly enthusiastic.

Responses from Readers

Calvin Arsenia: "I feel blessed."

Christopher Leitch: "[I am] honored to read from and about the incomparable Molière tonight."

Stuart Carden: "This is what my face does whilst acting Molière… such fun!"

Consuelo Cruz: "A great party that included readings of some of his best/funniest works, with locals you may recognize."

Responses from the Audience

Stephanie Roberts: "[The] night was terrific."

Carla Noack: "[It was a] wonderful evening."

William Eckhardt: "The public probably thinks of Molière as academic, but those readings were really fun."

Phil Smith, reluctant Molière inductee: "Molière – not nearly as bad as Shakespeare."

Birthday guests
(Photo: Felicia Londré)

It was a Birthday Party fit for a King. With bigger ones to come.

And just like at the Court of Bourbon nearly four centuries ago, alliances were forged, plans were hatched, minds were expanded.

Molière had made his mark.

L to R: Sarah Ingram-Eiser and Pat Williams (Photo: Felicia Londré)

Harvey Williams, Rashida Phillips, and Consuelo Cruz enjoying lively debates (Photo: Felicia Londré)

Fred Homan
(Photo: Felicia Londré)

L to R: Zach Moores as THE PHILOSOPHY
MASTER and Stuart Carden as MONSIEUR
JOURDAIN, reading from composite of
translations by Morris Bishop, John Wood,
Donald Frame, Felicia Londré of *The
Would-Be Gentleman*
(Photo: Felicia Londré)

L to R: Cyprienne Simchowitz as FROSINE and Sean O'Harrow as LA FLECHE, reading from *L'Avare*, translated by Albert Bermel as *The Miser*, read in both French and English (Photo: Felicia Londré)

L to R: Becky Smith and Peregrine Honig (Photo: Felicia Londré)

On the morning of Tuesday, February 11, 2020, Felicia sent an email to the Board that the assistant had submitted her three-month resignation notice. This was the beginning of personnel changes to the organization.

L'Espoire
Hope

Patricia (Pat) Hamarstrom Williams was a genuine *tour de force* as an international film and theatre producer/director and new media expert. She possessed an extraordinary intelligence, having had academic experience which included Harvard and the University Paris-Sorbonne, which made her familiar with Molière. Pat was a natural leader with a strong vision which came from her national commercial producing/directing clients including Michelob, Dr Pepper, American Airlines, AT&T, Holiday Inns, and the Southwestern Bell Pioneer Museum. She also was the chair at The Art Institute of Dallas where she was a new media curriculum co-writer of the system animation/multimedia/media arts programs and various Arts & Humanities classes.

In short, Chantal surmised, Pat was better equipped than she to assume a co-chair position on the Press and Publication Committee. So, she stepped down as co-chair to make way for a more talented individual.

In January and February 2020, news began to spread of a new infectious disease called COVID-19, or coronavirus, after the "crown-like" spikes on the outer layer of the virus.

Felicia followed up with Cynthia about her search for an updated interpretation of a Molière play which she and Damron had discussed at the Diastole several months earlier. Cynthia was perfect for the Thoroughly Modern Molière committee. She had been with the Unicorn Theatre, Kansas City's progressive theatre house, for more than 43 years, serving as a director, actor, designer, or producer for more than 300 productions of plays which normally would never see the light of day in a mainstream house. She took those years of experience and spent hours pushing the call for new interpretations through the national New Play Network, in addition to her own professional network.

Cynthia, with her short, curly-black hair and pink-framed glasses, could give Felicia a run for her money with her energy and determination, and both women would beat the Energizer Bunny in a race. Yet the response to her call for new plays was beyond underwhelming—it was spirit-crushingly devastating.

"I tell you, Felicia, the call barely managed a blip on anyone's screen," Cynthia informed the President.

"Ah, I'm not surprised. The Classics still have much to teach us, and we learn better from our mistakes when they are seen through the lens of history."

Cynthia, however, was not to be deterred, and true to her word, by January 2020, the Unicorn Theatre had commissioned Kansas City playwright, Natalie Liccardello, along with her sister Talia in Colorado, to write a play. Ted Swetz was brought in for script development and as the director; everyone began workshopping the new work a mere 11 months later.

Meanwhile, as winter bloomed into a more colorful season, both educational committees focused on the need for printed materials, such as programming brochures and study guides for French and theatre teachers for the 2021/22 school year.

Indeed, things were coming together nicely when French President Emmanuel Macron declared in militant language, "*Nous sommes en guerre* (We are at war)." On March 16, 2020, he ordered French citizens to stay in their homes in order to curtail the rapidly spreading corona virus. Halfway around the world, the San Francisco Bay area enacted the United States' first shelter-in-place orders. Initially, Macron's orders were for 15 days, which would, in theory, still allow Dr. Virginie Roche-Tiengo, a world-renowned Molière expert, to give her much-anticipated lecture, "From Louis XIV's France to the Anglophone World Today: Molière's Continuing Inspiration," on April 30 at the Kansas City Library.

IN *Kansas City* had already published the announcement of Dr. Roche-Tiengo's lecture in its April 2020 edition.

Arts & Culture IN KC
BY Judith Fertig

MAKE IT MOLIÈRE

YOU KNOW YOU'VE MADE IT when you're known by just one name: Homer, Shakespeare, even Cher. The international star known as Molière was an unlikely crossover hit, spanning languages and cultures. His work has been translated into every living language. Born Jean-Baptiste Poquelin in 1622, he took the stage name Molière as a playwright, actor, and poet.

Almost 400 years later, "KC MOlière: 400 in 2022, Inc." kicks off a multi-year celebration of the playwright's birth. "We also celebrate Kansas City's French founders who established a foothold here and fostered cordial relations with the Osage people in 1821," says Felicia Hardison Londré, president of KC MOlière: 400 in 2022, Inc.

Virginie Roche-Tiengo, an international Molière theater expert, kicks things off at the Kansas City Public Library Plaza Branch with "From Louis XIV's France to the Anglophone World Today: Molière's Continuing Inspiration." Anglophone studies focus on the challenges of taking a native language in theater and translating to the English-speaking world.

A reception on Thursday, April 30, begins at 6:00 p.m. and the lecture at 6:30 p.m. Reservations can be made at **kclibrary.org/signature-events**

Reprinted with the kind permission of *IN Kansas City*

As people began to physically distance themselves from one another on both coasts, the Board of **KC MOlière: 400 in 2022** welcomed French Cultural Attaché Tanguy Accart of the Consulate General of France in Chicago for his planned four-day visit to Kansas City, March 11-13, 2020. Felicia relished discussing the festival with him and the Board over lunch.

"Both the Chicago and New York consulates are interested in what is happening and are looking for ways to support your festival," Tanguy divulged. "They're especially interested in how Molière's work resonates with everyday American audiences. The Molière spirit is everywhere."

Felicia was beside herself with excitement. She completely agreed with Tanguy that the way to draw Americans in was through modernization of Molière's work. She felt many who might otherwise love the French playwright would be turned off by period-accurate costumes.

"His insights about our human foibles that are continually exposed through our politicians, and the fact that his commentaries are comedies rather than lectures, will further reverberate with audiences," Felicia affirmed.

"We have plans," Cyprienne said, picking up Felicia's conversational thread, "that all of the arts can have a place in this festival—such as dance and film."

"What you need, though, is some prominent French figure associated with your project," Tanguy suggested. "Perhaps a French director who could direct a Molière play in Kansas City? Or a leading French academic to participate in the preparation of French-American exhibits, conferences, workshops, museum events?"

L to R: Cyprienne Simchowitz and Tanguy Accart (Photo: Felicia Londré)

Cyprienne smiled, "Ah, Tanguy, we are already ahead of you. I've spoken with Jérôme Pouly of the *Comédie Française*, and he is quite interested. Between us, I think he may come here to help us celebrate on the actual birthday."

Sarah, the Vice-President, added that Dr. Roche-Tiengo would be coming as soon as France lifted its travel restrictions—surely this would all be done by the end of April!

Tanguy laughed good naturedly. "I should have known you were already working on this."

He was pleased to learn that Cyprienne had already been planning for international involvement, including arranging a June trip to Paris, and that the organization was taking smaller steps to garner media interest over a longer period of time.

Tanguy continued, "You need to be more strategic with your definition of the mission, as that will aid you in fundraising."

"That's not a bad idea," Jim, the Treasurer and Fundraising co-chair agreed. "It would help us formalize ties with some theatres, making them better partners."

As Tanguy's visit continued, more and more state governors began to issue orders prohibiting people from traveling and urging them to stay at home. On March 13, 2020, the President declared a nationwide emergency. Tanguy decided to head back to Chicago while travel was still an option. Two days later, the New York City public school system, the largest in the U.S., shut down to prevent the spread of the disease. Kansas City Mayor Quinton Lucas issued the order to shelter in place, effective 12:01 a.m., Tuesday, March 24. Kansas followed with a statewide order taking effect at 12:01 a.m., Monday, March 30 through Sunday, April 19. Missouri followed at 12:01 a.m. on Monday, April 6, 2020, until 11:59 p.m. on Friday, April 24, 2020.

Cyprienne and Felicia reconvened later and agreed that it was of paramount importance to have area theatres lock in some Molière plays for the 2021-2022 season or the French people would not think **KC MOlière: 400 in 2022** was worth their attention.

Pat sat behind her desk and stared at the blank Word document. She hated this part of the job—writing an uplifting opening article for the Summer 2020 newsletter. Her mind was in turmoil. How could she put a positive "spin" on what was happening? How could she take note of the horror while asking people to look ahead to what would be, hopefully, a better time?

Molière and the Pandemic
by **Patricia Williams**
Summer 2020 Newsletter, Vol. 3 No. 2

Like many arts and cultural organizations, **KC MOlière: 400 in 2022** has had to come to grips with the realities of an audience base trapped in self-quarantining practices demanded by the COVID-19 threat. It has forced us to re-imagine the delivery of our mission to introduce and educate local audiences to the mastery of Molière. Left without the venues of theatres and lecture halls, and needing to reach people in their homes, **KC MOlière: 400 in 2022** has embraced social media outlets and virtual meetings. This has presented all the challenges of new technologies and offered the rewards of opening up new delivery methods and audiences.

The centerpiece of our initiative has been the Five-Minute Molière video series. These short and entertaining instructions on Molière and his work are delivered by **KC MOlière: 400 in 2022** President Dr. Felicia Londré. Her talks generate enthusiasm for her subject as she creates warm images of theatre sugarplums "dancing in our heads." As one viewer put it, "I would listen to this woman talk about anything!"

KC MOlière: 400 in 2022 is hosting a watch party.
5 mins · 🌐

Dinner with Molière! Felicia Londré discusses Le Bourgeois gentilhomme with some bonus content-- this Five Minute Molière is 8 minutes long,... See More

5:43

⭐ WATCH PARTY

Video 4 Five Minute Molière: Le Bourgeois gentilhomme

⎙ Shop Now

www.kcmoliere400in2022.com

The Five-Minute Molière videos were Pat and Chantal's idea to connect with people while remaining physically distant. It was their job to transport Felicia into the 21st century through video recordings on a finicky computer which rarely wanted to cooperate.

Felicia fretted that videos were not exactly five minutes as the name implied. She rehearsed to get the pacing and her thoughts in order. Pat attempted to reassure her that if she went a few minutes over, no one would particularly notice. Chantal said it didn't matter, since she could do some very minor editing; nothing fancy, mind you. This failed to make Felicia feel better, really, because of the technological issues with the computer. Sometimes recordings would simply disappear and all their hard work would be gone. As they worked together, Chantal found they could have Zoom meetings and record them. Ultimately, the computer decided to work, and Felicia was able to record on her own, uploading her videos to the festival's Google drive for Chantal and Pat to disseminate.

On April 11, 2020, the Five-Minute Molière series debuted. Pat uploaded the videos to the organization's YouTube channel, KC Molière. She was also able to determine how to schedule Facebook Watch Parties on Monday, Thursday, and Saturday nights as she wanted to have a more social experience for a younger audience.

Top L to R: Richard Rischard, Chantal Roberts, Felicia Londré; bottom L to R: Jeff Jefferson, Becky Smith, Jennifer Martin (Photo: Chantal Roberts)

It certainly would not be a true cocooning experience without the invocation of Molière Zoom Rooms. Chantal Roberts has conceived of and organized a Molière play reading book club. It just finished reading and discussing, *The Imaginary Invalid*. Next up on May 18 is the Richard Wilbur translation of Molière's *The Bungler*.

The "book club" was another of Chantal's ideas to keep the visibility of the group in people's minds and to stoke the fires of devotion to Molière.

Note to Self: Stop coming up with fantastic ideas, Chantal thought sourly as she was volunteered to head up the book club. I've never even been in a book club. I have no idea how to do this!

Top L to R: Felicia Londré, Chantal Roberts, Jennifer Martin; bottom L to R: Bryan LeBeau, Richard Rischar, Becky Smith (Photo: Chantal Roberts)

"The benefit of being Ruler of the Book Club is," Chantal paused for dramatic effect, "I get to choose some of the lesser-known plays such as *Dom Juan* and *George Dandin*."

The book club wasn't just a *salon* for discussion of Molière's literary works. On March 29, 2021, Mechele joined the book club to give a mini-lecture on *L'impromptu de Versailles* and discuss her Facebook Live series concerning her production of *Molière at Versailles*, which also appeared on KC MOlière's YouTube channel. Jennifer, a regular at the twice monthly meetings, gave impromptu lectures about the theatre on topics like blocking, lighting, and directing a play.

Chantal, Richard, and Felicia proved their chops as the pandemic and the book club ground on. There came to be a time when few "good" translations could be found for Molière's plays. Felicia came to the club in July 2020 and asked them to read the first act of her translation and adaptation of *Les Fâcheux*, which was usually translated as *The Bores*, but she had translated it as *The Pests*.

"The translation never made sense to me because it is really more about pesky people, not a worrisome person," Felicia explained the reasoning for her title.

Participants in the club encouraged Felicia to complete the translation, and on August 24, 2020, they read and discussed it.

"I was laughing hysterically," Chantal gushed, "because, and I don't know how you would get permission from her, but when La Montagne is saying 'Shake-shake-shakin' about the dust on the hat? OMG, I could only think of Taylor Swift's song "Shake It Off." It would be *so funny* if he's in the back part of the stage, shaking the hat, like in Taylor Swift's video."

Felicia, being from an earlier generation, had called to mind Irving Berlin's song, "Shakin' the Blues Away."

"One thing that was interesting was the use of the phrase 'spic and span,'" Richard added. "I think of it as a more modern turn of phrase from the 1940s."

Richard Rischar, a music historian, choir conductor, and theater composer at the University of Michigan-Dearborn, and a guest artist at the Interlochen Arts Academy, routinely discussed Lully, a 17th-century composer who worked closely—for a while—with Molière. One of their most famous collaborations debuted on October 14, 1670, *Le bourgeois gentilhomme*. Lully and Molière created the *comédie-ballet* in *Les Fâcheux*, which reached its apex in *Le bourgeois gentilhomme*.

"I don't," Chantal rebutted. "Don't you remember the Spic and Span sponges? I remember my mom cleaning with them. Oh, maybe that makes me old…"

Richard decided to translate *Le Médecin volant*, often translated as *The Flying Doctor*, and offer it as *Chase-Scene Doctor* for classroom use. The book club discussed Richard's translation on March 15, 2021, and on the same day, Dani Trebus emailed 700+ local teachers the K-12 newsletter, in which she mentioned the availability of the new translation.

"I mean, I loved this, and I can see why it's perfect for 12-year-olds," Chantal said. "If I were directing it, I think I'd have something like Mountain Dew, when they're talking about pee; and I could just see the actor playing Sganarelle! Jumping through the window and down again to play the valet. Your translation played really well in my head."

Chase-Scene Doctor was offered on the **KC MOlière: 400 in 2022** website for teachers to use, but unfortunately, schools were still struggling with Zoom attendance. COVID cases had spiked again since winter, and there were no school plays for proud parents to attend. By May 2021, everyone was "Zoom'ed" out, and the book club had its last meeting.

Les Nouvelles Choses
New Things

Felicia wrote, "I love the great big countdown visible to everyone on our website. It generates much needed *oomph* to motivate our committee members, as well as generating excitement for the average person who is visiting our page."

As the country shut down in the spring of 2020 and people stayed home due to the pandemic, their rage began to show. This was the time of George Floyd's arrest and subsequent death, Jacob Blake's shooting by a police officer, and a failure to charge the officers who shot Breonna Taylor in her home. Protests erupted over the United States' systemic racism and police brutality. Americans began to look at their history and their culpability in furthering the systemic racism.

On June 9, 2020, Felicia pondered, "Does anyone know the right playwright who could write a one-act play, very short like a sketch, featuring the character of François Chouteau in some kind of exchange—perhaps with the Osage people, telling them what was entertainment in France? With no more than two or three additional characters, during the course of which he would say something about what a great comic writer Molière was?"

"We should take a minute and address a larger issue," Chantal interjected. "A Native American might be better as a playwright. I'm just thinking that we're having protests about Blacks being marginalized. Should we not use a Native American if we're talking about them? I mean, the Europeans did the same thing to the original landowners—the Osage. Why should a Euro-American write about what the Indigenous Peoples thought about another European?"

"Why didn't I think of my dear beloved friend/former student Philip blue owl Hooser? He is Choctaw, and he is a playwright! He has been going through a very difficult period. I will reach out to him. Philip authored *Coyote Mischief Tales*, which premiered at The Coterie, followed by performances at the Smithsonian Theatre,

Washington D.C., Philadelphia Theatre Caravan, and Johnson County Community College.

"And he's perfect because his comic voice goes from sly to sophisticated to literary wit to groan-inducing puns. Who better to channel the spirit of Molière?

"Thank you, Chantal! You are, as always, amazing!"

On July 8, the Board commissioned Philip to begin working on *Tartuffenthrope! Crossing Cultures with Chouteau and the Osage*, a 30-minute play suitable for outdoor performances, since no one knew when physical distancing requirements would be lifted. The play, set in 1821 at the confluence of the Missouri and Kansas rivers, focused on François Chouteau, his wife, and his brother bumbling their attempts to explain French culture to the Osage leader, Standing Bear, by performing re-membered sequences from Molière's "best play." Hilarity ensued because each of the three was doing a different play. Standing Bear intervened to help them sort out their personal differences even before they could deal with the artistic chaos. While the Chouteau Fountain dedication, which Felicia and Chantal had visited in November, was the impetus for this project, Felicia was most pleased that Philip's play would be available for school assembly performances during fall semester of 2021. The goal of **KC MOlière: 400 in 2022** always had been to combine education with entertainment and outreach to schools with large populations of minority students.

The stay-at-home orders were lifted for Missouri and Kansas in late spring 2020, but most people continued to stay home. New methods of communication and interacting were discovered. Most notably, Zoom.

Reprinted with the kind permission of Nicole Marie Green.

On Sunday July 26, **KC MOlière: 400 in 2022** debuted the world premiere performance of *The Miser*, newly translated by Nicholas Henke. Nick was a writer and theatre scholar who'd been forced to return to the US after living in France, due to COVID.

Top L to R: Collin Vorbeck, Nicole Green and Andy Perkins; bottom: Nick Henke
(Photo: Felicia Londré)

KC MOlière: 400 in 2022 partnered with Nicole Marie Green's Sunday Script Circle, which offered local actors (and non-actors) the occasion to read, unrehearsed, a play and then talk about it afterward.

"Community and mutual support were always my objectives," Nicole said, "because we are all starving for togetherness and theatre. This is a great way to do it and help the playwright hear how the words sound when they are spoken."

In a change from her usual, cold readings, Nicole pre-cast *The Miser*, which gave the performers the chance to rehearse if they chose. The talent pool featured local actor, Walter Coppage transformed into Harpagon, with Yetunde Felix, Allison Jones, Darrington Clark, Justin Barron, Tim Marks, Callie Fabec, Jake Golliher, Andy Perkins, Nicole Marie Green, Jacob Downing, Deanna Mazdra, and Chloe Robbins all working their magic. Maya Jackson, from Washington, D.C., was by far the audience favorite as the scene-stealing Frozine. Ryan Berstein handled stage directions while Collin Vorbeck was the dramaturg.

Collin and Nicholas offered insights and discussion points before and after the play and gave audience members a chance to interact with the actors in a way traditional theatre never had done.

The pandemic had not released its grip on the public. Regardless, *Blind Faith*, the commissioned play from the Unicorn Theatre, debuted a preliminary, livestream reading on Sunday, February 21, 2021, via Zoom. The reading allowed the Liccardello sisters and Ted to hear the words out loud and in a quasi-formal space with interaction from the audience, much like the Sunday Script Circle had done for Nick's new translation of *The Miser*.

Without knowing what the pandemic would do for the fall of 2020, the Board continued to move forward with its educational plans for the schools. Trudie Homan, of the Visual and Popular Arts Committee, contacted several illustrators regarding a children's coloring book. Originally envisioned as a learning tool for children who are too young to read and understand Molière's plays, the coloring book morphed into another trend of the time: an adult coloring book.

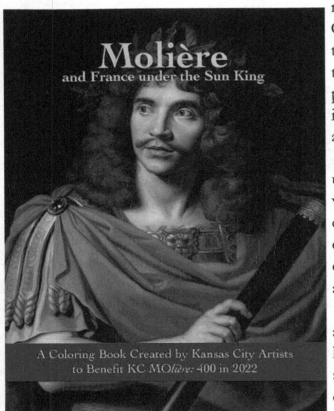

Front cover of the coloring book

However, Trudie and Beth were unsuccessful in finding illustrators willing to donate their time and drawings to a nonprofit for a long-dead playwright they'd never heard of and which would not bring them any kind of recognition.

The Press and Publications and Social committees lent helping hands to their sister committee in its search; Chantal, remembering the difficulty in obtaining a job out of university with no experience—yet remaining unable to get experience because no one would hire her—proposed a win-win scenario to the Kansas City Art Institute students: submit their drawings free of charge, be published locally in a coloring book, and be able to list that experience on their CV as real-world experience. The gamble paid off, as Brigid Elbert and Wes Parrill submitted photos; they also recommended another artist, Kelly Brown, who was studying painting and art history at the University of Kansas. Additional artists, including Sascha Groschang, Julia Brand, Karen Lisondra, and Peregrine Honig, also donated their time and talent to the book.

Sarah Ingram-Eiser connected the group with Words by Jen, a graphic design company out of Branfield, Connecticut. Jen Payne rescued the project by formatting the book, creating the cover design, obtaining the ISBN registration, and performing the other business associated with publication. It was clear that the coloring book would never break even through sales, but it sold well enough and provided an extra dimension of visibility. By June 1, 2021, the book was available on Amazon and in local bookstores. It was a nice prestige item to enhance mailings to French dignitaries.

While the flurry of activities continued in the committees, Becky and Felicia worked in the background to line up a Kansas City celebrity roster of readers for Molière's 399th Zoom birthday party on January 15, 2021. Felicia was acutely aware the celebration was only seven months away from the start of the 2021/22 events, and to date, they had been unable to widen the reach and visibility of the festival. The majority of emails, Zoom gatherings, and newsletters hovered around 100 participants, despite purchasing mailing lists, personal outreach, and news releases.

Indeed, Felicia had even attempted to entice city councilmembers in her December 14, 2020, email outlining what the organization brought to the city:

 Three professional play premieres would be offered in the 2021/22 season: an African American version of *Sganarelle* at KC Melting Pot, a commissioned work; *Mademoiselle Molière* at the Unicorn; and *Tartuffenthrope! Crossing Cultures with Chouteau and the Osage*, by Philip blue owl Hooser, to debut at the François Chouteau and Native American Heritage Fountain event on 24 July with subsequent touring to schools.

 René Bollier, André's Confiserie Suisse, would launch *The Molière*, a new *pâtisserie* featuring ingredients favored by Louis XIV, the Sun King of 17th-century France.

 Molière-label wine and coffee would be released to coincide with the new pastry.

Ten Kansas City artists contributed drawings to the Molière coloring book, to be published in early 2021. It includes a coloring page for Chouteau and two for Osage, as sculpted on the François Chouteau and Native American Heritage Fountain.

On a cold, blustery winter's night, despite the fact that *Tartuffenthrope! Crossing Cultures with Chouteau and the Osage* was still a work in progress, Charles Bruffy played François Chouteau, while Daisy Bücket portrayed Bérénice Chouteau, the mother of Kansas City, capping off the birthday event with élan.

YouTube thumbnail for the 399th birthday party
(captured by Jim Weitzel)

Becky, *organistrice de la soirée*, recruited some of Kansas City's glitterati to read English translations and the same passages in French. Nicole Marie Green adroitly controlled the Zoom room, and Chantal worked the "backstage" area by direct messaging the readers to be in their places so the momentum of the party could proceed with nary a dip in the pace. And so the 399th birthday party was in the books.

L'Ecole
School

Education during the pandemic had taken a toll on teachers at all levels, and the two educational committees of **KC MOlière: 400 in 2022** stepped in to help. Calan Welder, in the PhD program at Texas Tech University, helped the K-12 Committee formulate the announcement/rules for the 2021/22 Molière essay competition, *Jeu de Plume*. This was a play on the 17th-century phrase, *jeu de paume*, an indoor tennis court, which served as the theatre where Molière's troupe began in Paris. The committee hoped the essay competition would help local French teachers make Molière more accessible to their students.

Jeu de Plume.

Essay Contest

Felicia was disappointed. Because teachers were overwhelmed and exhausted, the *Jeu de Plume* essay-writing competition, even with its cash awards, failed to receive entries from high school students. She hated to do it, but she and the K-12 Committee decided to extend the deadline for submissions in the hopes of generating some interest. Ultimately, the project was rescued by Catherine Rush Thompson's connections with Rockhurst University French students, whose essays were published on the event website.

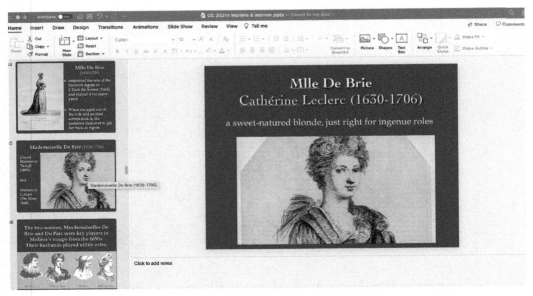

Screenshot by Felicia Londré of her PowerPoint slides

But Felicia was looking forward to the four-session Cockefair Chair course offered by UMKC. She enjoyed the lectures because the participants committed to them for the joy of learning and nothing else. Felicia herself would be presenting "Celebrating Molière's 400th Birthday" on February 24, 2021, to 28 virtual spectators. This allowed a larger audience to receive information about the **KC MOlière: 400 in 2022** mission and its connection with Kansas City's French origins. Felicia giggled. As Chantal would say, "It's all part of my 'evil plan' to entice the world with Moliere's life and his favorite theme: hypocrisy, encompassing fake doctors and zealots who made a show of piety." Of course, Molière opened himself up to mockery, as well, since the women in his life gave him plenty of material for his plays. For one thing, his marriage to a woman only half his age made him a target for criticism.

Molière's breakthrough moment which—for better or worse—consolidated his relationship with the Sun King, Louis XIV, was the infamous night at Vaux-le-Vicomte on August 17, 1661. It was there that Molière premiered *Les Fâcheux*, and Felicia was excited to be discussing this with the group at the second Cockefair lecture.

The week preceding Spring Break 2021 also proved unusual; the weather teased of Spring with temperatures hovering in the upper 60s. The Higher Education Committee announced Molière production commitments from Avila University, Kansas State University, Kansas City Kansas Community College, Northwest Missouri State University-Maryville, Missouri Valley College, and UMKC.

The **KC MOlière: 400 in 2022**'s volunteers sighed with relief and felt lightheaded because they hadn't even realized they'd been holding their collective breath.

The event they had been pushing and pulling everyone toward for three years was officially on the books. This was a big sign that their hard work was paying off. If it were permissible, they would have hugged one another. Unfortunately, there was still a pandemic to conquer.

The K-12 Committee, under the steadying hand of Martin English and Dani Trebus, held a reception in June 2021 to help teachers raise awareness of the organization's educational resources and to announce Molière-related events for the fall. The gathering at Kansas City Young Audiences introduced and honored the 10 Kansas City artists who had donated their talents to the Molière coloring book, which had been released a few days previously.

L to R: Jennifer Martin and Trudie Homan
(Photo: Felicia Londré)

Martin and Dani had been attempting to herd the cats that encompassed the Kansas City metroplex's school systems with monthly newsletters and entertaining, novel ways to teach culture and history to the students. They wanted to make the teachers' jobs easier. The event website offered teaching resources and information about the plays available for hire, such as:

- ***Tartuffenthrope! Crossing Cultures with Chouteau and the Osage*** is a short comedy by Philip blue owl Hooser (Choctaw). After its premiere on 24 July 2021, among the public festivities at the opening of the Chouteau and Native American Heritage Fountain, the play will be available for touring to schools. The play shows French fur traders in 1821 attempting to explain French culture to the Osage by acting snippets from Molière's work, but they bungle their performance hilariously.

- UMKC's **Mobile Moliere: The Long Path Players** is a 45-minute performance for middle and high school audiences, available on selected dates from October 4 to 22, 2021. What happens when modern-day actors take on the roles of a 16th Century Italian traveling troupe? **Commedia** Chaos! UMKC Theatre's MFA actors bring their riotous romp of a touring show to local schools, performing up-to-date adaptations of Molière scenes and characters including Pantalone, Arlecchino and Molière himself!

- **Make 'em Laugh! A Commedia dell'Arte Demonstration on the Enduring Humor of a Classic Form** is a one-person 45-minute performance/demonstration focusing on **Commedia dell'Arte**. Educator, actor and creator Stephanie Roberts will perform an entertaining and educational presentation about the history and practice of the classic Italian theatre form **Commedia dell'Arte**.

The pandemic hurt everyone irrevocably. Despite educational outreach initiatives, the Zoom school year pushed students' learning backward, and teachers were forced to make up for lost time. They couldn't take on anything extra during the pandemic, and afterward, most school administrators worried about assembly-room gatherings. Teachers were too worn-out to push for these theatre presentations, even at a nominal fee.

Jennifer was able to give a master class at Kansas City Kansas Community College (KCKCC) entitled *Molière in Style: A Master Class in Baroque Movement Style*—a workshop about the complex rules of behavior modeled on the court of Louis XIV demonstrating the courtly bows and curtseys, fan codes, snuff-taking, and guidelines for standing, sitting, and walking. All of which were satirized in Molière's fops.

Front: Jennifer Martin teaching KCKCC students
(Photo: Gary Mosby)

Actors, Brittany (Welch) Crooke, Jenise Cook, and Eileen Dixon in UMKC's *Mobile Molière: The Long Path Players* with Felicia Londré, second from right
(Photo: Stephanie Roberts)

Stephanie Roberts had a measure of success in October 2021 with UMKC's *Mobile Molière: The Long Path Players*. As a UMKC associate professor of theatre, Stephanie was the ideal director and leader, due to her extensive experience in the art of comedy and, particularly Molière-appropriate, *commedia dell'arte* techniques and traditions, which was highly physical, comedic work for the students who had been training for two years. She also recruited The Coterie Theatre's artistic director, Jeff Church, to help with obtaining an impressive roster of October school bookings for the touring group.

L'Anticipation
Anticipation

The weather on Monday, February 8, 2021, was the kind of cold that gets into your bones and never leaves. The high temperature was 9 degrees Fahrenheit, which was the reason, everyone in Kansas City knew, the Chiefs had lost to the Tampa Bay Buccaneers the night before, even though the game was held in Tampa. *Obviously*, Patrick Mahomes had been channeling the city's pain.

Later Monday afternoon, Felicia, Cyprienne, and Sarah Ingram-Eiser, Vice-President of the Board, blessed technology for their Zoom meeting with Julián Zugazagoitia and Anne Manning to discuss the possibility of holding the 400th birthday at the Nelson-Atkins Museum of Art in Kirkwood Hall. Sarah's longstanding, prestigious connections to the Nelson-Atkins Museum made her the perfect liaison to the museum's events planner, Nichele Anderson, during the weeks of proposals, negotiations, and revised proposals before a contract was signed.

Original reading of *The Pests* by KCAT (Photo: Felicia Londré screenshot)

Inspired by the reception the book club attendees had given her, Felicia took their suggestions to heart and spoke with John Rensenhouse of the Kansas City Actor's Theatre about a possible production. John, a veteran of Broadway productions and Artistic Chair of KCAT, spotted a winning script in *The Pests*. He grabbed some of Kansas City's favorite local actors, including Walter Coppage, who read in *The Miser* for the Sunday Script Circle, Vi Tran, Bri Woods, Robert Gibby Brand, Meredith Wolf, and Matt Schwader and put together the world-premiere reading of the new adaption, again via Zoom, on March 7, 2021. KCAT generously donated the profits to **KC MOlière: 400 in 2022** and gave an honorarium to the actors and director, most of whom were still out of work due to the continuing theatre closures.

As the pandemic wore on, the days gradually got warmer and longer, and on April 19, it seemed that Felicia and Kip's dreams were finally taking shape. The Board of **KC MOlière: 400 in 2022** signed a contract with Nelson-Atkins Museum of Art for Molière's 400th birthday celebration on January 15, 2022. Planning the festivities—and, more important, the cake—could begin!

"It is funny," mused Becky, who was helping the Social Committee order the food, "how we use to blow all over cakes and then eat them, but now we wear masks and shrink from people who sneeze." Determining how to deliver cake for all partygoers was a chore for someone's to-do list, in addition to raising the ante for an even more spectacular birthday celebration.

Approximately 10 months earlier, Becky had invited Jean-Charles Foyer, a St. Louis historian who lived in France, into the mix, since the pandemic had brought him home to the States. Jean-Charles was the type of man who would make a Jane Austen heroine swoon, and it was initially hoped he could record a Five-Minute Molière, since he was well known in Kansas City for his playful historical costume re-enactments. Chantal had talked with him about the recordings, and learned, unfortunately, that he was headed back to France as soon as the borders reopened, however briefly, in 2020. Jean-Charles was still dedicated to the mission, though; he was one of the stars who read Molière in the original French as well as the same sequence in English for the 399th birthday party—all the way from Paris. And when asked, he gladly said he would be the *Maître des Cérémonies* for the grand *fête*.

Chantal and Felicia were pleased, but for different reasons, even though it was over the same subject. Philip was making progress on *Tartuffenthrope! Crossing Cultures with Chouteau and the Osage*, and the Board retained a Native American, Nathan Bowman, to direct the play. This was another way to incorporate indigenous voices when walking the fine line about the Europeans who'd busted onto the scene in the 18th and 19th centuries, attempting to "give culture" to the Native Americans. Since he and Phil were Native Americans, both were equipped to write and direct the play.

Nathan, who had co-founded and was Producing Artistic Director of the Kansas City Public Theatre, knew the play would first be debuted at the unveiling of the Chouteau monument, where Felicia and Chantal had attended the groundbreaking nearly a year earlier. Nathan had worked extensively with outdoor productions and brought a wealth of expertise to this project.

Workshopping *Tartuffenthrope*. L to R: Elena Nguyen, director Nathan Bowman, Derek Trautwein, (standing) Don Dagenais, Georgianna Buchanan, (standing) Felica Londré, Brian Duskey, writer Philip blue owl Hooser, (front) Kitty Corum
(Photo: Jennifer Martin)

"My initial instinct is to create as much of an actual Molière play as possible. I want it to feel like it is a Molière piece, but I also want to maintain this balance that Phil strikes so well," Nathan told the actors during their workshop. "Even though I'm Wyandotte, and Phil is Choctaw, I don't want it to seem like the French are just here to teach the Natives 'high culture' and how we are appreciative for these things.

"The stories Molière tells not only have a timelessness to them that everyone comments on, but they have a cross-culturalness, too. Phil does a really good job of showing that, despite two completely different backgrounds, we never want it to seem we are saying one culture is superior or supplants the other."

Nathan went on to instruct the actors, "The character of Standing Bear gets a lot to say, and we get to hear his perspective, so I think the script walks that balance. As I approach this with you, I want to make sure we maintain that balance. After all, encounters between Native Americans and French fur trappers were all contemporary events with Molière in the mid-1600s—not that the Chouteaus were contemporaries of Molière; they were not. But the Chouteaus started in St. Louis, which was obviously a French city, so they likely had some knowledge of theatre."

Nathan smiled, "At least that's the story we're going with in this play."

Spools
(Photo: Georgianna Londré Buchanan)

June 5 wasn't only the reception for teachers, but also the debut of MoMo, the mascot Molière figure who drew his name from the first letters of Molière's name and the postal code abbreviation for Missouri, as in KC MO*lière*. It was serendipitous that MoMo, Molière's nickname, appeared in an adolescent girl's illustrated diary, complete with French teenage slang in Cécile Alix's book *Molière vu par un ado*. And it was thought the perfect way to entice teachers to use the services offered by the organization.

As Felicia's daughter, Georgianna Londré Buchanan grew up in the theatre. A well-respected costume designer who worked at half-a-dozen theatre companies and contributed to more than 300 shows in the greater Kansas City metroplex area, Georgianna used her skills to bring Molière to life for public appearances in 17th-century court-approved fashion.

Georgianna volunteered her talent and labor to create MoMo's mascot head of closed-cell EVA foam, to which she added a wig constructed with tubular horsehair, and later a more wearable velvety brown fabric hair. Having created numerous animal costumes for The Coterie over the years, Georgianna was well experienced at working with the sculptural elements in costume.

She studied the many portraits of Molière as well as fashions of the period to design the mascot's clothes. Her design was based on middle-class fashions of the mid-17th century. Although Molière appeared frequently at the court of Louis XIV in the 1660s, he never adopted the excess laces and ribbons of the more pretentious courtiers.

Georgianna complained to her parents over their weekly Sunday lunch, "I mean, we know from his portraits and others' descriptions that he had a dark-ish complexion with full lips, and usually a *moustache* that suited the com-

Georgianna Londré Buchanan
(Photo: Selfie)

ic roles he played. But I can't get any information on the color of his eyes. The portraits aren't consistent." Ultimately, everyone decided to go with hazel eyes for the mascot.

Chantal's mobile rang on the evening of June 24, 2021. She saw that the caller ID said Felicia and said, "Hello," but heard nothing but sobbing on the other end of the line.

"Felicia, what's wrong? What happened?" Chantal's heart began to race, thinking the worst, that perhaps a family member had passed away.

It was equally devastating news, as Felicia again gave a short sigh and said, "Oh, Chantal, Sarah has died."

Sarah Frances Foresman Ingram-Eiser
(November 7, 1936 - June 24, 2021)
Soror, Ave Atque Vale
By Felicia Londré
Fall 2021 Newsletter Vol. 4 No. 3

Sarah Ingram-Eiser, founding Vice President of **KC MOlière: 400 in 2022**, passed away on 24 June. We mourn the loss of this vibrant personality who gave so much during her two full years on our board. We celebrate the time we had with her.

So ready to help with any little task was she that we little suspected how many other arts organizations were also getting the benefit of Sarah's hands-on contributions. Elizabeth Kirsch's *In Memoriam* in *KC Studio* XIII, 5 (September-October 2021, p. 34) and the *Kansas City STAR* obituary (15 July 2021, p. 7a) list 25 or so of the music, dance, theatre, visual art, political, church, health, financial, women's, and neighborhood groups to which she gave her time and effort. A memorial service was held on 29 August at Grace and Holy Trinity Cathedral where her ashes were placed in the Memorial Garden.

Sarah was a major presence at our season announcement and teacher appreciation party at Kansas City Young Audiences on 5 June. She brought the fruit punches and the ice and helped sell our *Molière and France under the Sun King* coloring books, a project which she had been instrumental in bringing to fruition. Besides serving on the Fundraising Committee, Sarah took on the role of Judgemeister, coordinating the panels of judges of different age groups for our K-12 *Jeu de Plume* essay competition.

At our board meeting on Monday, 7 June, Sarah volunteered to take the 8 a.m. shift at Kansas City's Bicentennial Day and Dedication of the Chouteau Fountain on 24 July. And suddenly on 13 June, her daughter Alli Ingram-Eiser Sifers took her to the KU Heart Center. Alli reported that when Sarah was wheeled out of surgery, she commented that they ought to be selling our *Molière* coloring books there!

Many have reminisced about Sarah's famous dinner parties, and I was lucky enough to be invited out of the blue to a dinner at her house even though we had never met. She had a visitor from California, Barbara Oliver, with academic theatre connections, and Sarah thought we should meet. It was a lovely, memorable occasion. Several years later, Sarah and I happened to sit next to each other at a matinee performance of *A Soldier's Play* at Black Repertory Theatre of Kansas City. She wrote her phone number on the back of one of my cards, and it was that very card that jumped out of my rolodex when I was wondering who should be asked to serve on the board of the newly formed nonprofit. When I called to ask if she would be vice president, her first question was, "How's your health?" as she did not want to have to move into the president position. What a lucky break for us that Sarah accepted!

Sarah's close connections with the Nelson-Atkins Museum of Art (she called it her "second home") served us well when it became our venue of choice for Molière's 400th birthday party. Sarah took over the contract negotiations for us. She brought her tape measure the day we went to envision the party layout in Kirkwood Hall and enthused about our project to the young museum attendant who wondered why we were shuffling about on the floor with

L to R: Sarah and Jim
(Photo: Felicia Londré)

her 16-foot-long tape. She motivated me to make the two-sided informational cards that we use as handouts and should have had in our bags to give to that young man!

One of the things that most struck me about Sarah as I was getting to know her was how easily she could relate to anyone. When Tanguy Accart, the cultural attaché for the French Consul General in Chicago, visited Kansas City on the eve of the pandemic in March 2020, we had a French luncheon for him and the board and representatives of the International Committee. Later, when I received my photos of the lunch from the printer, it was amazing to see how totally engaged Sarah was in each of the photos of her. She was completely, actively focused on the person in conversation with her. Her dynamic charisma virtually popped out of the photos in a way I had never seen in all my years of taking snapshots.

If I needed to consult Sarah about something, I learned that it was best to call her around 9 a.m. It was such a morale-booster just to hear her answer the phone with her cheerful, ever-upbeat "Good morning." When the calls went unanswered that week of 13 June, it was deeply unsettling. Patricia Cleary Miller told me Sarah was in the hospital and kept me updated. Of course, we fully expected she would be back with us, as vibrant as ever.

Beyond these personal memories, I'd like to share a few of the many tributes of sympathy that came to **KC MOlière: 400 in 2022** over the next weeks.

Nichele Anderson: Although I've only connected with Sarah a few times, I fully felt the passion and vibrancy that she radiated.

Victoria Botero: Sarah was a remarkable woman and blessing to all!

Steve Paul: I didn't know Sarah very well, but over many years she was always kind to me and we had quite a few jolly encounters.

Stephanie Roberts: What a loss to our arts community.

Bobbie Jeffrey: She was a woman who invested so much in the arts and who will be deeply missed by her community, family, and friends. A life well lived.

Sidonie Garrett: She was a wonderful ally and straight talker, ever pragmatic and kind. And energized! Sarah will be much missed throughout our community.

Richard Rischar: We truly do work on the shoulders of such giants, and to their memory we will endeavor to make greater and more inclusive art.

Sarah Ingram-Eiser, *soror, ave atque vale.*

On advance!
Onward

I don't understand. I knew she was in the hospital, but the last I heard she was released."

Chantal was confused. The organization had come through the pandemic. They were set to debut *Tartuffenthrope* at the Chouteau and Native American Heritage Fountain in a month to the day of Sarah's passing. Yes, they had reached out to many organizations for collaborations, such as a Missouri bicentennial-promoted ice cream social, which fizzled; and yes, they still struggled with getting the mainstream media to pay attention, but surely, they were moving forward.

A few weeks had passed since Sarah's untimely death, when Felicia rallied the remaining Board members to fill the empty post of vice president. True to her journalistic form, Becky politely declined the role, as she felt she was more useful as a Board Member at Large. Don, who had shepherded Felicia through the process of the 501C(3) paperwork, graciously took point on July 8. Don was a never-ending source of help. He took on the solo chairmanship of both fundraising and overseeing finances. Felicia murmured a prayer to the theatre gods that he and treasurer, Jim Weitzel, were longtime friends. Don continued with the small but time-consuming and/or expensive things every organization needs, like printing 200 letterhead envelopes on his home printer, giving fundraising pep talks at events, and liaising with music organizations. Jennifer Martin and Dorothée Werner were added as board members.

Jennifer was keeping the Board up to date with the gratifying news that, from Columbia, Missouri, to Manhattan, Kansas, colleges and universities were scheduling Molière productions. Even in spite of the challenges COVID posed to live performance!

Dorothée was the Honorary President of the Alliance Française de Kansas City, and working in partnership with Cyprienne to bring attention to the organization in France, which believed, correctly or not, that it had a monopoly on its national treasure.

Philip and Nathan had put the final touches on the commissioned play about Kansas City's origins in 1821, with the Chouteaus attempting to remember and convey what they learned about Molière in school to the Osage. They managed to whittle it down to 30 minutes, perfect for school-age attention spans.

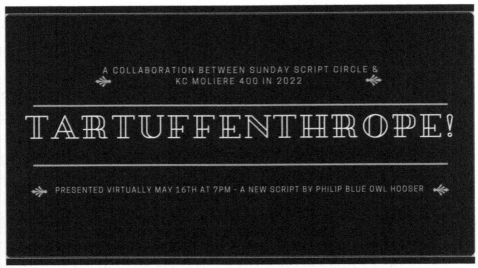

Reprinted with the kind permission of Nicole Marie Green

In another first, Nicole Marie Green's Sunday Script Circle collaborated with **KC MOlière: 400 in 2022** to present *Tartuffenthrope! Crossing Cultures with Chouteau and the Osage* virtually. This dress rehearsal allowed Philip, Nathan, and the actors to hear the pacing of the actions and adjust accordingly for the world premiere of the play at the François Chouteau and Native American Heritage Fountain dedication activities on July 24, 2021.

L to R: Derek Trautwein, Kitty Corum, Brian Duskey (Photo: Felicia Londré)

L to R: Nathan Bowman, Kitty Corum (Photo: Felicia Londré)

On July 24, 2021, at 11 A.M. *Tartuffenthrope! Crossing Cultures with Chouteau and the Osage* premiered on stage for the first time on what had to have been the hottest day of the year to that point.

"It's, like, Arkansas hot," Chantal complained to the other volunteers under the tent where the organization sold its coloring books and handed out teaching resources to passers-by. As much as she loved MoMo (and she *adored* MoMo), she felt very sorry for him (or her, Chantal guessed, as it could have been a woman in the costume—and she forbade Georgianna or Felicia from telling her since it would ruin the fun and mystery) because she was suffering in the heat wearing just a t-shirt, shorts, and a sun hat; she could not imagine what the actor playing MoMo must have felt like under all that foam. Although her empa-

Top L to R: Dani Trebus, Jim Weitzel, Felicia Londré; Bottom front: Pat Williams; Bottom back: Becky Smith

thy did not stop Chantal from closely eyeballing those she suspected might have been playing MoMo.

MoMo with the Media
(Photo: Felicia Londré)

No, Venne looked too calm and cool. True, MoMo would go sit in the car with the AC on full blast (Chantal didn't know whose car…) from time to time, but Venne was, as always, impeccably dressed—she would have used the word "dapper." Neither was it Georgianna, because Chantal had seen both MoMo and her together. No, she just didn't know who it was, which tickled her to no end.

MoMo turned up repeatedly at **KC MOlière: 400 in 2022** functions and even had the media, ultimately, wanting to take photos with him.

Georgianna was pleased that MoMo was becoming a much-loved personality at the local festivals, and the Board hoped he could eventually meet his mascot-counterpart, Good Will, at the Heart of America Shakespeare Festival. Unfortunately, the stars did not align for the two playwrights to meet, as the pandemic kept the Heart of America Shakespeare Festival closed for 2020-21.

MoMo says, "VOTE FOR TARTUFFENTHROPE!"

Despite premiering on July 24, 2021, *Tartuffenthrope!* managed to slide right under the July 30 nomination deadline and ended up a finalist in *The Pitch*'s Best Play of Kansas City 2021. It was simply a shame, lamented everyone involved in the project, that not one school had picked up Tartuffenthrope! Out of everything **KC MOlière: 400 in 2022** had done, Philip's play was garnering the most attention from local media.

In July alone, there were three news pieces in both print and radio media about Philip and his play. In August, *Kansas City Magazine* interviewed Philip about the backstory of the play and how it came to be.

Commençons
We're Starting

August 13, 2021, was the official beginning of the **KC MOlière: 400 in 2022** festival, and the Kansas City Baroque Ensemble gave a concert at Visitation Catholic Church titled *Molière's Versailles*, with music from composers who were Molière's contemporaries. It was the first time the ensemble was able to perform together since the start of the pandemic, and Trilla Ray-Carter wrote, tongue in cheek, in the program that she invited three *gentilhommes* vocalists, Jay Carter (countertenor), Jacob Sentgeorge (tenor), and Gabriel Lewis-O'Connor (bass), who sung works by Marc-Antoine Charpentier. French masters Pierre

L to R: Felicia Londré, Chantal Roberts, and Becky Smith

Beauchamp and Jean-Baptiste Lully, whom Richard had discussed in the book club, were also represented, showcasing music that was as pompous and powerful as Louis XIV himself.

The Master of Ceremonies was Robert Gibby Brand, a classical music lover and professional actor who had appeared on almost every stage in the Kansas City metroplex.

"I assure you," Robert addressed the audience with a smile, "that although tonight's concert opens with *Le ballet de la nuit*, we will not be playing the entire ***13-hour*** *oeuvre*, which started at 6 p.m. in Versailles when it was debuted and went until a final series of dances in which the Sun King appeared as Apollo rising up with the sun the next morning!"

A collective sigh of relief was heard, although muffled, through the attendees' masks. Most were simply giddy to be able to meet in person, inside, for the first time in a year-and-a-half.

It was especially thrilling to hear Marc-Antoine Charpentier's *Magnificat à trois voix d'hommes* sung by the three harmonized voices. As well as

L to R: Robert Gibby Brand, singer, and Trilla Ray-Carter
(Photo: Felicia Londré)

to hear a suite from *Les fâcheux*, about which Chantal and Becky had been learning so much over the past few months.

A reception with wines donated by the White-Simchowitz Family Charitable Fund followed the concert. Fred Homan took his station, the ever-faithful bartender, and for that Felicia was grateful. Making sure cups were filled and plates were full was a thankless task many volunteers didn't want to undertake, but she could always rely on Fred, who had been the bartender for the volunteer party at the Diastole and the 398th birthday party at the KC Melting Pot Theatre. What made Fred even more amazing was the fact he was on the ever-useful Press and Publication Committee, the workhorse of the festival, along with Pat, Becky, Catherine, Fred, and Chantal, who were always willing to volunteer or help a sister committee.

L to R: Venne Londré, Robert Gibby Brand

In late April, Becky and Felicia were treated to a tour of André's Confiserie Suisse by René Bollier, Executive Pastry Chef and Chocolatier. With enthusiasm and verve that would have heartened Kip, Felicia had convinced René to create a dessert exclusively for the festival.

The confection, a mini Bundt-shaped almond cake with candied orange peels covered in André's signature dark chocolate, proved thoroughly enticing to everyone. In de-

L to R: Becky Smith, Amanda Davison, Doug Frost, René Bollier (Photo: Felicia Londré)

scribing his motivation, Bollier referenced the orange grove beloved by Louis XIV, as well as the popularity of almond and chocolate at the Royal Court.

In a coup, Becky landed Doug Frost, one of only three people *in the world*, to have achieved the dual designations of Master of Wine and Master Sommelier. Doug, an open and welcoming man, was already a good friend to the organization, having generously donated wine to the 398th birthday party celebration. Doug was immediately intrigued with the idea of crafting a fortified dessert wine to accompany André's Confiserie Suisse's *The Molière* pastry.

Doug cleverly married the Traminette and Valvin Muscat grapes from Missouri in collaboration with Les Bourgeois Vineyards to create *Joie de Molière*. The grapes were developed by Cornell University with a sweetness that didn't lend itself to becoming cloying on the palate like syrup.

At the invitation-only debut party under the *porte cochère* at the Kemper Museum of Contemporary Art, Chantal and Doug talked about his inspiration, and he admitted, "I *did* base the wine off my preferences."

"I don't blame you. I'd have done the same," confided Chantal, "I skipped the coffee to get to you first. Besides I like wine better than coffee!"

Vice President, Don Dagenais, doesn't know which to try first:
The Molière or *Joie de Molière*
(Photo: Felicia Londré)

September 29 was still broiling. The only benefit of the heat, thought Chantal, who cursed herself for changing handbags and not packing her fan, was that the event could be held outside and thus allow everyone to physically distance from one another.

L to R: Felicia Londré, Becky Smith, Chantal Roberts, Pat Williams, Jennifer Martin, Don Dagenais

As fall fell, there was a fast and furious onslaught of plays and lectures, just as Felicia had imagined.

Chantal, for one, was desperate to get tickets to see Stephanie's *Mobile Molière*, and was terrified the show would sell out on both nights, since there were still COVID restrictions on how many people could attend indoor events. She knew she could probably beg to be let in, or again, ride in on Felicia's good graces, but she still considered herself new and didn't want to take advantage of people's charity.

Third-year MFA actors from UMKC, Jenise Cook, Eileen Dixon, Riley Lucas, Michael T. Oakes, and Brittany (Welch) Crooke, began working with UMKC theatre professor, Stephanie Roberts, at the beginning of Spring Semester 2021. They found that Molière's themes were timeless, but as young adults, they couldn't overcome some of the situations, such as the beating of servants, fathers bartering their daughters into marriage, etc.—the group resolved itself to creating a modern adaptation. At least

Actors, Michael T. Oakes and Brittany (Welch) Crooke in *Mobile Molière*. Reprinted with the kind permission of Stephanie Roberts.

until they began digging into Molière's one-act plays, which captivated their imaginations as they remembered, not so long ago, their experiences in high school when adults attempted to appear "cool" to teenagers. The actors quickly shifted their outlook, and rather than do an entire play, created a "Greatest Hits" montage from Molière's most famous plays.

On tour, each student wore a number of hats, both literally and figuratively. In addition to playing numerous characters, they took turns being tour managers, school liaisons, props and costume coordinators, and drivers. Felicia was so pleased with the fast-paced performance, which evoked

L to R: Jenise Cook, Eileen Dixon, Riley Lucas, Brittany (Welch) Crooke. Reprinted with the kind permission of Stephanie Roberts.

93

L to R: Becky Smith, Jim Weitzel, Felicia Londré (back), Alli Jordan being presented with the Consulat's grant (Photo: Beth Bryant)

what she imagined what 17th century theatre might originally have been like. The actors, no more than students themselves, hit their marks in pantomime and facial by-play perfectly.

Mobile Molière performed 11 shows total: two at the Coterie, two at UMKC and seven shows in six schools. Unlike with *Tartuffenthrope!*, Stephanie was able to obtain a few bookings at schools such as St. James Academy, University Academy, and Frontier STEM, which were able to take advantage of the new Molière-inspired play from October 4-14, 2021.

As the UMKC's Mobile Molière: Long Path Players discovered, it was difficult for teachers to engage the students in Molière's timeless themes when the conveyance of the themes was outdated. Alli Jordan and Tracy Terstriep-Herber, teachers at Pembroke Hill School, overcame this through a grant from the *Consulat Général de France*. On October 23/24, 2021, the pair presented *A Molière Fête: Then and Now*, a pair of one-act plays, to a limited audience of mostly Pembroke Hill School parents and selected guests. Act I was traditional Molière with *The Precious Young Ladies*, set in the fashionable Parisian salon of Gorgibus, father to Madelon and uncle to Cathos. The setting and costumes of the Pembroke production cleverly evoked the atmosphere of 17th-century France in all its excess.

Alli, the recipient of the grant, wrote the second one-act play, *The Precious Young Men*, which was set in a contemporary bar called The Poets Pour House, complete with a stage for poetry

Playbill design: Grace Weber. Reprinted with the kind permission of Tracy Terstriep-Herber.

slam competitions. Tracy, head of Pembroke Hill School's theatre department, produced, directed, and choreographed the two shows.

Alli and Tracy took pains to highlight the parallels in action and characters as the plot unfolded in these two very different worlds. In Molière's world, the women spurn the men who attempt to court them with their poetry; at The Poets Pour House, it is the men, believing themselves to be cutting-edge poets, who spurn the women.

The cultural values and clothing of the suitors were another parallel that helped the students understand Molière's material. In Act I, the suitors seek revenge upon the ladies who have slighted them. Dressing their servants as aristocrats so that the ladies will take notice, the men then expose, in a very public manner, how shallow the woman are by revealing the women are only attracted to the servants because they think the servants are aristocrats. In the counterpart act, the fashion-conscious ladies transform themselves into *avant-garde* poets who dress in second-hand clothing with no makeup and messy, dirty hair. The ladies then reveal their true selves, and the men are superbly shamed by their own mannerisms.

Becky stood off to the side of the stage, as she was wont to do, shunning the spotlight, in amazement at the courage and moxie it took the students and Alli to put themselves out to the world, opening themselves up for criticism. She was especially impressed to see the "kids"—because even Alli was young enough to be called a "kid" despite being an adult—going after their passions. At the end of the play, Jim, and Felicia were thrilled to give Alli the honorarium.

he Kansas City Museum, originally Robert Alexander Long's home, built in 1907

L'Automne
Autumn

J and taking up a city block (3.5 acres) on Gladstone Boulevard, and its staircase were the dramatic backdrop for Dr. Henriette Runte's November 19, 2021, lecture, Molière and Me, connecting her personal history to that of Molière.

Both Dr. Runte and Molière share the same birthday; both had parents who urged them to pursue "sensible" careers (Molière: law; Dr. Runte: medicine); both rejected their parents' advice because their grandfathers instilled in them a love for the theatre. Becky was spellbound by Dr. Runte's energy during her presentation, which contained a number of dramatic, quick-change costume ensembles underlying her flair for fashion and flamboyant clothes. For an academic, Dr. Runte surprised Becky, who thought she could have been an actress with the way she enacted scenes and captivated the imagination with the personal stories of how Molière had occupied such a large part of her life.

L to R: MoMo and Dr. Henriette Runte on the stairs of the Kansas City Museum.
Reprinted with the kind permission of the museum.

MoMo, in his ever-flirtatious style, was able to participate in Dr. Runte's lecture while she discussed *The Precious Young Ladies* (*Les Précieuses Ridicules*), the very play Pembroke Hill School students had performed a month earlier. MoMo helped her up the grand staircase in their 17th-century clothing as she laughed at the character's pretentiousness, such as calling a chair a "commodity for conversation."

L to R: Dr. Henriette Runt with MoMo on the stairs of the Kansas City Museum. Reprinted with the kind permission of the museum.

The entire audience was charmed, and the lecture was a great success, thanks to Paul Gutiérrez for making the space available even though the pandemic numbers had been increasing due to people being indoors, in-person classes, and re-laxed mask mandates. If the trend from the previous fall continued, the unthinkable might have to be considered: cancellation of the birthday party.

Dr. Mechele Leon, co-chair of the Higher Education Committee with Dr. Jennifer Martin, presented at the UMKC Emeritus College Annual Dinner and Program on the topic of *Molière as National Hero*.

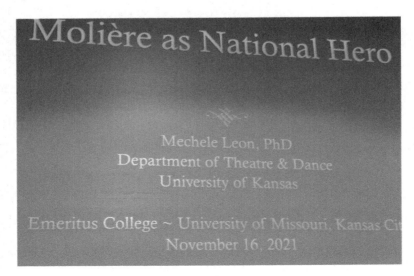

Jennifer introduced Mechele, who in addition to being a theatre professor at the University of Kansas, is also the author of *Molière, the French Revolution, & the Theatrical Afterlife*. There's no doubt Molière would have been proud of how

the revolutionaries challenged the status quo and wrested him from a monopoly allowing new theatres to produce his work. Molière was, after all, before his time in giving the women of his troupe equal pay and say in his first theatre company.

Jennifer and Mechele had contacted all area colleges and universities to promote and coordinate the 2021/22 season's scheduling of plays by Molière in Kansas and Missouri their theatre programs with some success, which also brought the much-desired press and media attention the festival had been striving for.

The universities' 2021/22 theatre season kicked off in November with Freyda Thomas'

Dr. Mechele Leon

translation of *The Learned Ladies* (*Les Femmes savantes*) at William Jewell College and Richard Wilbur's translation of *The Imaginary Cuckold* (*Sganarelle, ou le Cocu imaginaire*) at Avila University.

Chris McCoy directed the Jewell Theatre Company in a stylized approach, with costumes by Scotty Wiggins that had the title characters wearing period-evoking cages over their skirts, as if to say that their yearning for a life of the mind might be a way to overcome social constraints on women. Their enormous folding fans were used to perfection, snapping rhythmically to punctuate the action and dialogue.

Cast of *The Learned Ladies*
(Photo: Facebook post from Jewell Theatre Company)

Andrew Ivy as Trissotin (the name means "three times foolish") added some over-the-top physicality to the verve of his line delivery. Paige Wright put some heart into the domineering Philaminte, while her beleaguered husband Chrysale (Jaimeson Satterfield) nailed Molière's favorite schtick, going back and forth between resolve and weakness. In a uniformly strong cast, London Eichelberger's Martine and Isabel Warden's Vadius made special impact.

That same Molière schtick popped up again in David Zamora's centerpiece monologue delivered by Sganarelle, the title character in Avila University's *The Imaginary Cuckold*. In heroic mode, he donned armor and knee-guards. Matt Schwader Harbor directed the colorful romp, imaginatively costumed by Shannon Smith-Regnier. Avila's take on the short comedy included live musicians and a *commedia dell'arte* sequence that echoed the comic mix-up.

Tyler Lindquist designed the fanciful set and played the young lover Lélie as a charmingly puffed-up hero. Isabella Brauner, as the rubber-glove-wearing maid, combined common sense and fun as she dealt with clever confusions and helped the ingenue Célie (Danielle Adcock) reconcile with Lélie.

One month from the 400th birthday, on December 12, 2021, the Unicorn Theatre presented the one-night-only, world-premiere professional reading of the first English-language translation of *Mademoiselle Molière* by Gérard Savoisien.

Unicorn Theatre Hosts a Thoroughly Modern Molière Reading
by **Rebecca Smith**
Winter Interim 2022 Newsletter Vol. 5 No. 1

L to R: Stephanie Roberts, Felicia Londré,
Cynthia Levin, Sophiko Tsabadze,
Vi Tran, Amy Attaway
(Photo: Chantal Roberts)

It's been two years since the Unicorn Theatre has been able to hold one of its regular Sunday evening in-person readings—we were thrilled to be the first back.

Mademoiselle Molière, directed by **Stephanie Roberts**, who gave us the successful *Mobile Molière* in October, was performed December 12, kicking off the Unicorn's return and kicking off **Molière**'s 400th birthday year.

It was a very engaged crowd of a hundred or so that followed the 2018 words of **Gérard Savoisien** imagining the ups and downs of the relationship between Molière and his companion/muse, **Madeleine Béjart**.

L to R: Vi Tran, Amy Attaway
(Photo: Chantal Roberts)

Beautifully directed by Roberts, actors **Vi Tran** and **Amy Attaway** convincingly flirted, coasted, erupted, and heartbreakingly reconciled over the 80 minutes. As in most Molière plays, there was considerable laughter and wit but also great poignancy and sadness. It was a look at the playwright not often portrayed – the brilliant, innovative, lovable Molière as unfaithful heartbreaker. The steadfast devotion between the two was clear, but his roving eye and vulnerability to the "new," young, and tasty was ultimately destructive.

A goal of KC MOlière: 400 in 2022 has been to contemporize the master, and what could bring him into a current context more effectively than this displayed susceptibility to a pretty form and the resulting mayhem? Also striking a chord was Madeleine's complaint that Molière was "toadying". She urged him to "be true" and not let himself become a "laughing stock".

Madeleine was certainly the heart of the play, but Molière was not treated villainously. He was weak, to be sure, but his thorough charm, sincere love for Madeleine, and own personal chagrin shone through.

So – it was a real success for writer, director, and actors. But no less was the success of the translator, our own **Dr. Felicia Londré**. This was the first English interpretation and staging of the play, and she proved ideally up to the task. Had she lived in the 17th century, Dr. Londré could have undoubtedly been as productive a match to Molière as Madeleine.

L to R: Felicia Londré and Cynthia Levin
in the talk-back
(Photo: Chantal Roberts)

After the reading a lively talk-back ensued, led by Unicorn Executive Director **Cynthia Levin**, and the audience appreciation was evident.

For the "human" and "universal" nature of the play. For its historical references. For its entertainment value. There's every reason to consider mounting it as a full production and that idea will, we hope, be under discussion. The original, after all, won Best Play in a Private venue (*sic*) in France.

In the play, Madeleine and Molière are reviewing their relationship in 1661. They acknowledge they are in danger of falling "into the hornet's nest."

Does anyone argue that we have fallen into one ourselves? "Are we in a play?" as voiced in the reading, is a question that must occur to all of us at one time or another.

It was all hands on deck, as there was less than a month to go until the apex of the festival—the 400th birthday—arrived. Daily, Felicia sent a bevy of emails to the Board and the volunteers.

"Consul Général Yannick Tagand notified us that the French Ambassador and his wife had made plans to attend the festivities," Felicia emailed the Board and Chantal. "This is a Very. Big. Deal."

Felicia was beside herself because she had drawn up an itinerary for showing the foreign visitors the attractions of Kansas City, but it was not to be. "Well, at least the silver lining is that it will be easier for us not to have to worry about finding French-speaking volunteers to chauffeur them around town."

Yannick suggested that the most important thing was to get even more press attention—something that the Board didn't need to be told twice. The Press and Publication Committee had been fighting that losing battle for three years.

Then on the morning of January 5, 2022, just 10 days before the event, Julián Zugazagoitia, director and CEO of The Nelson-Atkins Museum of Art—the venue where the party would take place—called Felicia with the bombshell piece of news that would change everything.

Bonjour, Kansas City
Hello, Kansas City

So, you see, the museum must take responsibility for the safety of the whole community. Given the numbers of museum staff who are out with Covid, it might even be necessary to close the museum tomorrow," Julián said with a sigh as he rubbed his eyes, although Felicia could not see this through the telephone.

She could, however, hear the fatigue and defeat in his voice.

"Some galleries have already been closed because of a shortage of guards. We've even cancelled a fundraising event in February. Cancelling yours is not something we do lightly."

Julián had just come from a briefing at the Kansas University Medical Center, which spelled out the alarming increase in COVID numbers in no uncertain terms.

"Perhaps I've been rereading *Oedipus* too often, but I've learned that one can't rebel against Fate," Felicia spoke softly; her mind already creating the email with the To-Do List for the volunteers.

"Molière has waited 400 years already, so he can hold out a bit longer," Julián promised. "Perhaps I used the wrong word with 'cancel;' it is really a postponement. Let's get together in a few weeks and determine when the celebration will be. Numbers always seem to drop in the late spring and summer."

Molière can hold out, Felicia thought bitterly, but from her perspective, she was counting the days to be rid of all the cartons, including 100 black berets for the volunteers, a transparent face mask for *Maître des Cérémonies* Jean-Charles Foyer, 150 folding fans and 100 handkerchiefs for the period movement demonstration, crayons and coloring pages for the children's corner, nametags with our logo, nametag holders and pens, not to mention the door prize items, all of which were clogging her back hall…

Like Pat in the summer of 2020, Felicia sat in front of a blank computer screen. She was in a state of zombie-like shock; she smiled ruefully. Chantal would be amused at that image.

"This is truly hard to take after our accelerating build-up of readiness," Felicia wrote to the volunteers, giving them their marching orders:

 Becky: Cancel the cake.

 Don: Alert the Shepherd's Center volunteers.

 Jim: Cancel the order of Molière cakes from André.

 Dorothée: Let the Académie Lafayette singers and their parents know.

Felicia hoped the French dignitaries would still be able to come for the World War I Museum and Opening Night of *The Pests*, uniquely aligned with Molière's birthday of Saturday, January 15, but she had not yet heard from the Consul General's office.

Finding the best date for a rescheduled event was of paramount consideration. The weekend of April 30-May 2 would be ideal because of landing *Comédie-Française* superstar, Jérôme Pouly. And if the French Ambassador and his wife could not attend opening night of *The Pests*, then at least in May it would, presumably, be warm enough for an outdoor performance of *Tartuffenthrope!*—one of Felicia's dearest hopes.

Perhaps, thought Chantal, Fate wasn't punishing them for their hubris, because beginning in the late hours of January 14, 2022, it began to snow. The snow continued through until 6 p.m. the following night; had they held the festival, people would not have shown up, Chantal feared, since no one really would want to drive in this kind of weather for a playwright they had never heard of, even with the promise of free cake.

Chantal was thrilled to have tickets to Kansas City Actors Theatre's full production of *The Pests* (*Les Fâcheux*), which had been informally read in Nicole's Sunday Script Circle and in the book club. She was also grateful to her husband, a native Iowan accustomed to driving in snowy, wasteland, tundras, who'd agreed to haul her to the City Stage at Union Station so that she might see the play. She was surprised the theatre was packed despite the weather and wondered if her initial apology for Fate had been incorrect.

L to R: Cyprienne Simchowitz, Felicia Londré, John Rensenhouse (Photo: Venne Londré)

For the theatrical production, Matt Schwader was the director. Chantal was pleased to see some of the actors who had become her favorites over the course of the pandemic, such as Vi Tran, who had done several readings in the script circles and Robert Gibby Brand from the Baroque concert ensemble.

She was, however, disappointed that no one undertook her advice about the harried valet singing "Shake It Off" when cleaning his master's hat. Their loss, really. She was also

L to R: Matt Schwader, Georgianna Buchanan, Felicia Londré (Photo: Venne Londré)

disappointed she could not attend the Really Cool After Party with Actors, but there'd been an uptick in COVID cases, and one could not be too careful.

Probably one of the best pieces of news about the three-week run was that, in the dead of winter, City Stage had a predominately full house—time after time audience members raved about how much the fun and frivolity had meant to them as an antidote to the dreary pandemic months and how the show lifted their spirits when they needed it most.

L to R:, Christina Schafer as Clymène, Jake Walker as Eraste, and
Chioma Anyanwu as Orante (Screenshot from YouTube promotion)

But what really thrilled Chantal, besides Felicia's talent with the clever rhyming scheme, were the outrageously choreographed movements by Ron Megee and the candy-like costuming by Georgianna. And then, she was not sure who to credit this to if the truth was to be known, Chantal's mind *exploded* at the musical numbers!

Um, hello? Rap? Meet Minuet. Minuet, Rap. Collaborate.

Artistic co-opting: priceless.

Actors in *The Pests* (Screenshot from YouTube promotion)

Then, Becky pointed out that the Nelson-Atkins had a very popular Manet painting, *The Croquet Party*. When out came the musical number, "We Used to Dress Up for Croquet," which harkened back to the fact that *Les Fâcheaux* was a *comedie-ballet*, Chantal whispered this fact to her husband; he probably didn't really care and she also probably annoyed the audience members sitting around her.

Actor and theatre professor Cinnamon Schultz directed Kansas City Kansas Community College's spring production of Ranjit Bolt's translation of *Tartuffe*. She understood that keeping the play to a length similar to that of a feature film was a desirable for today's audience attention span.

Becky particularly admired the set designed by Wendy Scott, which was reminiscent of the Dark Shadows gothic soap opera series with its large draperies, foreboding crosses, dark furniture, and walls expertly painted with *trompe d'oeil* penumbras. She felt it was a nod to a power-hungry, would-be oligarch who knows how to game the system. And for those who see through his charade, he bullies, plays the victim, and cries "fake news." It was, mused Becky, a perfect example of how Molière was still relevant today, despite the characters on stage wearing brocade, velvet, and corsets.

L to R: Alena Riley as Elmire and John Carver as Tartuffe
(Photo: Gary Mosby)

L to R: Alexander Josúe Aguirre as Orgon and Chloe Easley as Dorinne
(Photo: Gary Mosby)

TARTUFFE CHARACTER CHART

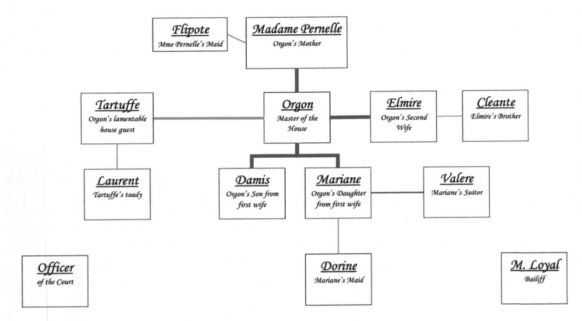

Chart of characters in Tartuffe by Kyn Johnson.
Reprinted with the kind permission of Kansas City Kansas Community College.

Reprinted with the kind permission of
Northwest Missouri State University and Kansas State University.

If you love *The Imaginary Invalid*, you get to see it **twice** in the month of April!

Both Northwest Missouri State University and Kansas State University will host showings of Molière's last play.

The hypochondriac Monsieur Argan has doctors visit his home every day, convinced he is suffering from a number of illnesses. His doctors, knowing he is perfectly healthy, prescribe him worthless medicines and procedures in order to dupe him out of his money. Argan wants his daughter, Angélique, to marry a doctor so he can save on his medical bills and always have a physician handy. But she's in love with someone else – the young, handsome Cléante. Complicating matters is Béline, Argan's scheming wife, who wants to send Angélique to a convent in order to profit from Argan's pension and savings, even before he is dead. Soon Toinette, Argan's saucy maid and nurse, and his pragmatic, kind brother Béralde join in a madcap scheme to save true love and find a way to help Argan give up the doctors for good.

Reprinted with kind permission of Northwest Missouri State University

An unseen benefit from the postponement of the birthday celebration was that several events all converged into what turned out to be Molière Week. The educational and social calendar for the festival was packed:

Friday, 29 April, 2 p.m.	Performance of scenes from Molière by Académie Lafayette students
Saturday, 30 April, 7:30 p.m.	Performance of *M de Molière* by Jérôme Pouly with reception afterward
Sunday, 1 May, 1 p.m.	Matinée performance of *M de Molière*
Sunday, 1 May, 2-4:30 p.m.	Celebration of Molière's 400th birthday at Nel-son-Atkins Museum
Monday, 2 May, 2:30-3:30 p.m.	Pouly in conversation with Rockhurst University and UMKC French students at Rockhurst
Monday, 2 May, 5 p.m.	Pouly's Zoom conversation from Kansas City to all branches of the Alliance Française
Tuesday, 3 May	Pouly's Q & A with Académie Lafayette and other school French classes
Tuesday, 3 May, 6:30 p.m.	Lecture on *Molière's Continued Inspiration* by Dr. Virginie Roche-Tiengo at the Plaza Library

The Consulat Général de France was very interested in **KC MOlière: 400 in 2022**'s educational objectives. They had granted $500 to Alli Jordan for her new play and an equal amount for the April 29, 2022, performance of scenes from Molière by students of the Académie Lafayette International High School in the theatre at the Oak Street campus. The performances encompassed scenes from Act 2 of *Les Fourberies de Scapin* directed by Mme Nora Abied; "Minuet" piano duo from *Le Bourgeois gentilhomme*; and scenes from Act 4 of *Tartuffe*, directed by Mme Kate Absher.

Cyprienne Simchowitz continued communications in her effort to bring the eminent *Comédie-Française* actor Jérôme Pouly to Kansas City for the culmination of the yearlong festival, along with their friend Dr. Virginie Roche-Tiengo of the Sorbonne Paris Nord.

L to R: Nour Nora Azar, Bob Paisley, Karen Paisley, and Catherine Tissot (Photo: Felicia Londré)

Bringing international attention to the often-overlooked Heartland was also the task of Catherine Tissot of the Alliance Française de Kansas City who soon took over the arrangements and found herself devoting whole days to the business dealings via email and Zoom. For nearly a year, she convened monthly Zoom meetings between Pouly in Paris with Cyprienne, Felicia, and herself in the small AFKC office. She made endless trips to the Warwick Theatre on Main Street, where METropolitan Ensemble Theatre had offered the most advantageous terms for presenting the world-premiere of Pouly's one-man play *M de Molière*. Catherine scrupulously monitored the budget, for which **KC MOlière: 400 in 2022** and AFKC pooled contributions.

When the planning was taking place with the Alliance Française, Felicia couldn't help but note, with a bit of *schadenfreude*, that the bicoastal branches of the Alliance were shocked and confused by the fact that the backwater, flyover states of Kansas and Missouri had snagged a *Comédie-Française* superstar. They could not possibly understand why a *sociétaire* would visit Kansas City and were fairly certain there were no direct international flights to the middle of nowhere. But of course, thought Felicia smugly, they didn't have Catherine and Cyprienne.

Chantal was in a state, or a pique, or she was fixin' to pitch a fit. (Proper Southern Ladies do not *have* fits; they *pitch* them.) She and her husband were on their way to see *M de Molière,* the one-man play about Molière at METropolitan Ensemble

Theatre's Warwick Theatre, and Aaron was driving around the block for the third time, looking for parking. On their third pass, they saw Felicia and Venne go into a door, which, had they not seen the Londrés use it, they would never have found the door.

L to R: Chantal and Aaron Roberts at *M de Molière* (Photo: Felicia Londré)

"Park right there!" Chantal commanded, as Aaron readied himself to go around a fourth time.

He immediately pulled into the empty spot, and Chantal was out of the car before he turned off the engine. They were not late, but she did not know where they were going and she did not see any reason to continue driving in circles when there was a perfectly serviceable parking spot *right there*. Chantal marched up to the hidden door, which now wasn't so hidden since it was at the top of a flight of metal stairs. Then she stopped, unsure of what to do. The door definitely did not look right. It was marked Service Entrance. Were they to go in the Service Entrance? Chantal could see that this was the entrance to the theatre's backstage. Which made sense. *Of course*, Felicia could use the Service Entrance. But Chantal? Not so much.

She turned around and began walking to her left and rounded the corner, only to find there was no access to a path to the front of the building. She and her husband were joined at this time by another couple, who were also looking for a way in. Walking a few doors further, they found an alleyway, which isn't at all sketchy, thought Chantal. They took the alley and popped out on Main Street. Another left found them at the front of the theatre and in the lobby. When Chantal turned to Aaron in a panic

Poster for *M de Molière*. Used with the kind permission of Nathalie Feldman.

and said, "The tickets! I left them in the car. Can you go get them? I'm wearing heels and can't walk fast."

It ended up being a needless panic, since they were allowed in because their names were on the attendee list, and they had their vaccination cards.

Comédie-Française Superstar to Perform in Kansas City
by Felicia Londré
Spring 2022 Newsletter Vol. 5 No. 2

One of **KC MOlière: 400 in 2022**'s three missions is to bring national and international attention to our city's world-class arts scene. Our active collaboration with the *Comédie-Française* in Paris achieves that goal beyond our wildest dreams.

Founded in 1680 with a core company of 27 actors from Molière's troupe and the other Paris troupe of the day, the *Comédie-Française* has remained a top destination in Paris for nearly three and a half centuries – with only a brief hiatus during the French Revolution, when half the company narrowly escaped the guillotine! During its 342-year existence, only 538 actors have attained the rank of *sociétaire*.

We are excited to announce that **Jérôme Pouly**, the 510th *sociétaire*, will premiere his one-man play, *M de Molière*, in Kansas City on 30 April and 1 May at the METropolitan Ensemble Theatre's Warwick Theatre. Later this year he will not only tour his play in France, but he will direct Molière's *Amphitryon* at the *Comédie-Française*. Currently he plays the title role in a C-F studio production of *George Dandin*, in which he played the servant Lubin during his first season, 1998/99, at the *Comédie-Française*.

M de Molière is a series of vignettes that build upon Molière's themes and comedies. Molière's "M" is the M of medical matters, misers and misanthropes, machinations, malady, malaise, malarky, Mascarille, mischief, music, melancholy, marriage, mendacity, morality, mortality – and more. Jérôme Pouly will perform in French and engage the audience in the choice of vignettes at each performance. **Dr. Virginie Roche-Tiengo** will assist with some commentary in English.

Pouly's distinguished career includes roles in ten productions of Molière plays. These include Sganarelle in *L'Ecole des maris* (*School for Husbands*), Cléonte in *Le Bourgeois Gentilhomme* (*The Would-be Gentleman*), Mercure in Amphitryon under the direction of renowned Russian director Anatoly Vassiliev and later the title role in another C-F production of *Amphitryon*, and various roles in Molière's *Dom Juan*, *Le Malade imaginaire*, *L'Avare*, *Le Mariage forcé*, and *La Jalousie du Barbouillé*.

Recently Pouly enlisted several of his colleagues, fellow *sociétaires* at the *Comédie-Française*, to make a short comic video titled *Hello, Kansas City*. The humor comes from cultural misunderstanding about Kansas City's French founders, the Chouteau family, and what they might have known about Molière. The video is in French with subtitles.

While the world premiere of Pouly's *M de Molière* and the *Hello, Kansas City* video from the *Comédie-Française* are stars in the crown of international visibility for our efforts, there has also been some great international press coverage, including a paragraph in *Le Monde* (31 December 2021, p.23)

The Kansas City premiere of *M de Molière* is co-produced by **KC MOlière: 400 in 2022** and the *Alliance Française de Kansas City* with generous support from the **White-Simchowitz Family Foundation Fund**. Performances will be at 7:30 P.M. on Saturday, 30 April and at 1 P.M. on Sunday, 1 May. Pouly's Sunday performance will end in time for him to join the 400th birthday festivities in Kirkwood Hall at the Nelson-Atkins Museum and be introduced there by **Cyprienne Simchowitz**. The birthday celebrations will continue on Tuesday, 3 May at 6:30 P.M. with a Kansas City Public Library Plaza Branch lecture by Dr. Roche-Tiengo on Molière's place in world literature and theatre.

Chantal was concerned that her husband would not enjoy the play. It was all in French, and if she were honest with herself, she did not know if she would understand it all—being that it was all in French. Aaron assured her that he would be fine, and she assured herself that Dr. Virginie Roche-Tiengo would be there to translate. She had paid to have the VIP tickets because this was a once-in-a-lifetime event, and so she and all the other VIPs were seated in the front row.

L to R: Some members from the audience, including Catherine Rush Thompson (front) and Felicia Londré (back), participated in the interactive show with Jérôme Pouly. (Photo: Chantal Roberts)

116

A scene from *The Would-Be Gentleman* brought audience members, including Blogger-In-Chief, Catherine, and, in what had to be a pre-arranged stunt, Felicia, onto the stage to repeat the vowel sounds taught by Pouly as the Philosopher. Somehow the lesson transitioned into a game of musical chairs by which the "losers" recovered their places in the audience. Pouly clearly savored Sganarelle's "tobacco" speech from *Dom Juan*, and he explained that Molière was not urging everyone to smoke but actually using a metaphor to extol the habit of theatre-going.

There were several costume changes and, at one point, Jérôme had difficulty getting his jacket on. Being a consummate actor with 20-plus years under his belt, he was familiar with situations when live theatre did not go as planned; actors train for such events. He walked calmly up to Aaron, turned around, and said, *"M'sieur, s'il vous plaît…"*

Jérôme Pouley
(Photo: Suzanne Kinner, reprinted with the kind permission of Pouly, Frédéric Gasnier
[*Cie Coeur et Panache*])

Without missing a beat, Aaron helped Jérôme into his coat, and the show went on with no one the wiser because there had already been audience participation—this was just another piece of schtick. But what happened later horrified Chantal: Jérôme, still speaking completely in French, came to stand in front of Aaron as he was pulling people onto the stage.

Imperceptible, so very faint, so very small was the head shake Aaron gave Jérôme that had she not been sitting directly next to them, Chantal would have missed it. Still speaking completely in French and never pausing, amused and amazed, Jérôme imperceptibly and faintly shook his head, too, but with a raised eyebrow. Aaron gave a curt nod. Continuing to speak only in French and never pausing, surprise flickering in his eyes for a millisecond, Jérôme moved on, and Chantal relaxed.

L to R: Catherine Tissot, Cyprienne Simchowitz, Jérôme Pouly, Felicia Londré, Nathalie Feldman, Virginie Roche-Tiengo. (Photo: Suzanne Kinner, reprinted with the kind permission of Ms. Kinner, Dr. Roche-Tiengo, Jérôme Pouly, Frédéric Gasnier [*Cie Coeur et Panache*], and Nathalie Feldman.)

There was the obligatory Really Cool After Party with Actors, which Chantal could have attended this time, and wanted to, but those at the party were mostly Alliance people whom she didn't know. Felicia, for her part, was in a state. There was so much to do and concentrate on that she barely had time to breathe. When Chantal and Aaron greeted Felicia earlier in the evening, before the show, Felicia barely recognized them—not because they looked so different, but because her mind was going in a million directions and she was finding it difficult to concentrate. Chantal recognized this mania because she had felt it, too, several times hosting events for important business clients she wanted desperately to impress and from whom she desperately sought approval. So, when Aaron suggested they head home, she reluctantly agreed because she neither wanted to distract Felicia nor stand against the wall waiting for someone to take pity and speak to her.

"It has taken four years, scores of volunteers, use of video meeting technology we didn't even knew existed until the pandemic to get us to this day," Felicia said to Venne.

"But we did it. We've had parties, school programs, concerts, lectures. A promo video—even a video salute from the *Comédie-Française*. International press coverage; a book club; 15 newsletters; a mascot. I don't think Kip or I originally envisioned a mascot," she said, smiling and taking maternal pride in Georgianna's handiwork.

Felicia continued to tick off the accomplishments as she donned the 17th century-inspired costume Georgianna had made for her, reminiscent of a noblewoman's brocade dress.

Poster. (Credit: Pat Williams and Lex Lamb)

"A Molière coloring book, which we had published on Amazon. André's *The Molière* cake; *Joie de Molière* dessert wine from Doug and Les Bourgeois Winery. And academic and professional stage productions all over Missouri and Kansas. I wish Kip had lived to see this!"

Felicia Londré being presented the Proclamation by Kansas City Councilman, Eric Bunch (Photo: Don Ipock)

Felicia was reciting these things to calm her nerves, for the Grand *Fête* was a few hours away. Volunteers were to arrive at 1 p.m. But something always goes awry when a big event is planned. They had already lost some volunteers. The Ambassador and his wife could no longer attend.

L to R: Becky Smith, Felicia Londré, and Lex Lamb
(Photo: Venne Londré)

When she arrived at the Nelson-Atkins, Felicia was planted to the spot, staring at all the boxes of accoutrements, including pages and crayons for the Children's Corner, handkerchiefs and fans for Tracy's dance number, programs, and gift bags for the presenters needed for the event. She was in dismay, wondering how she would get all of it to Kirkwood Hall without going through security several times. But then, as always, Becky appeared like a movie superhero emerging out of the mist at the split-second perfect moment, wearing her 17th-century maid costume and instantly picking up boxes to carry inside.

Chantal, for her part, didn't have an assigned role, and was a floating volunteer. She preferred flitting around to see where the problems were and swooping in to fix them so that Felicia could concentrate on other issues. One problem was that there were not enough chairs for all the attendees, and the museum could not, unfortunately, retrieve more.

"Hi. I wonder if I could ask a favor of you," Chantal leaned in and quietly whispered to a mother and father with their two children. "I have a woman with a broken foot and her companion. Can I get two of you to give up your seats for them?"

People were only happy to oblige, and when the infirmed woman and companion were ensconced in their seats, Chantal felt a hand on her arm. A woman had stopped her

L to R: Chantal Roberts, Professor Barb Trout of University of Nebraska at Lincoln
(Photo: Chantal Roberts)

Children enjoying the festivities
(Photo: Felicia Londré)

to say that she was a professor in historical costumes and dress, and she had never seen anyone so period-accurate in their reenactment. Chantal was, as the British would say, gobsmacked. It was truly the result of four years' research on Pinterest. But what struck Chantal as hysterical was the fact that she opted for the period-accurate "spaniel ears" hairstyle, which was, in her humble opinion, worse than the Big Hair of the 1980s. How women (and men) thought that was an attractive look was beyond her.

What also amused Chantal was Felicia's email after the event, thanking her for the photographs when she was on stage playing Musical Chairs at *M de Molière*.

"I have been neglecting to tell you how charming you and Jean-Charles looked together, as it appeared you were flirting at Versailles!" she gushed.

L to R: Chantal Roberts and Jean-Charles Foyer
(Photo: Don Ipock)

Chantal giggled. She remembered with vivid clarity what she and Jean-Charles were talking about: they were broiling hot under all those clothes! He was in a Napoléonic wool jacket, waistcoat, and shirt; she was in a chemise, stays, and a dress with wool stockings (because this party was supposed to take place in the winter and (a) Chantal hadn't wanted to be cold, and (b) she was too cheap to buy silk stockings, even though the party had been moved to the summer).

Lex, the administrative assistant, got her cardio exercise for the day running up and down the back stairs to the museum's basement to fetch the gift bags.

Former Kansas City Mayor Sly James (2011-2019)
giving welcoming speech to attendees
(Photo: Don Ipock)

A month earlier, with the gentle, diplomatic, helpful, nudges from Becky, Felicia invited Dr. Licia Clifton-James, a UMKC "triple-crown" winner who obtained her undergrad, masters, and Ph.D. at the university, and her husband to the birthday party. Former Kansas City Mayor, Sly James, an ardent supporter for the arts, and Licia's husband, would be the feather in Felicia's cap. In her 44 years of living in Kansas City, Mayor James was, by far, the most arts-supporting politician thus far. It probably came from being married to a professor with a Ph.D. in art history and the humanities consortium and who'd written her thesis on African and African-American art. Felicia was thrilled to learn that Mayor James and Dr.

Clifton-James would be in attendance—if only for a brief moment—to welcome everyone to Kansas City.

Board member Dorothée Werner stepped in at the eleventh hour to conduct the Académie Lafayette children singing « *Bon Anniversaire* » to Molière as Jean-Charles, the *Maître des Cérémonies,* cut the ceremonial cake in place of Yannick Tagand, whose flight had been cancelled at the last minute, preventing any French governmental representative from attending the party.

Regardless, the *fête* was a great success as there was standing room only in Kirkwood Hall. Jennifer Owen, of Owen Cox Dance, pirouetted gracefully in 17th-century balletic movements, and Tracy brought a few brave volunteers in front of

400th birthday cake
(Photo: Chantal Roberts)

the stage to demonstrate how to "minuet" and, correspondingly, flirt to maximum effect with fans and handkerchiefs, accompanied by members of the Kansas City Baroque Consortium, who had even brought their own harpsichord. Under the

Tracy Terstriep-Herber (center, back) teaches volunteers
how to dance and flirt (Photo: Don Ipock)

leadership of cellist Trilla Ray Carter, they created a 17th-century soundscape for the entire event.

Events always seem to have problems. If there was any hiccup to birthday *fête*, aside from the lack of seating—which Chantal solved by sneaking behind the dais and the retractable stanchions because she and Jean-Charles also did not flirt over how their feet were hurting—was the fact that the audience's mood had begun to shift. Long since tiring of being in their Children's Corner, and not at all interested in learning the minuet, the children had seen the cake being cut nearly 45 minutes earlier, and they still had not received ny cake. Thanks to the fast thinking of Venne, he and Chantal began passing out handkerchiefs and fans to the children to keep them quiet and entertained, but that, too, resulted in the issue of ever more children wanting the props.

L to R: Cyprienne Simchowitz, Jérôme Pouly, Nathalie Feldman
(Photo: Don Ipock, reprinted with the kind permission
of Mr. Ipock, Pouly, Frédéric Gasnier [*Cie Coeur et Panache*],
Dr. Roche-Tiengo, and Nathalie Feldman)

It seemed that the cake and refreshments were waiting for Jérôme to come from his matinée, which had started (and thus ended) late. Finally, the French superstar came rushing in, still in makeup and the elaborate brocade jacket from his show. Cyprienne translated his speech, and then there was cake.

Poster. (Credit: Pat Williams)

Two days later, Dr. Virginie Roche-Tiengo, from the Université de Paris-Sorbonne, gave a lecture entitled *From Louis XIV's France to the Anglophone World Today: Molière's Continuing Inspiration.*

"My heart is really bursting with the way Cyprienne has welcomed me to Kansas City," Dr. Roche-Tiengo started. "But as you will discover, no dream is beyond reach with Molière in the United States of America.

"Jean-Baptiste Poquelin Molière was born in the first arrondissement, in the heart of Paris, and here we are, 400 years later, celebrating his 400th birthday in the heart of Kansas City—in the heart of America."

After the lecture, Chantal and Venne walked out of the auditorium together.

"Felicia is going to have a fit until she knows how Virginie did that curtain effect in her PowerPoint," Venne confided.

"Oh, I missed it. I was stuck in traffic and arrived 15 minutes late."

"It will be on the library's YouTube channel. You'll have to watch it. It was fantastic." Venne stopped where there was a spread of appetizers and already a small gathering of Virginie, Cyprienne, and Felicia. Soon Jérôme and his wife, Nathalie, joined them. The entire gathering spoke softly in French.

June 3, 2022, saw the visit of another dignitary from the Consulat Général de France, Chicago, Nicolas Douay, Higher Education Attaché, along with the opening night of *Secrets & Lies*, a contemporary African American adaptation by Nicole Hodges Persley of Molière's *Sganarelle, ou le Cocu imaginaire*, which showed at the Kansas City Melting Pot Theatre. Nicole, who had fond memories of reading Molière while at The Université de Lyon II- École de Lumière and at the Université d'Avignon, decided to focus her play on a Black family with ties to France and West Africa, highlighting the African Diaspora in France. Nicole's vision adapted the play to address a lack of privacy in the social media age while a family wrestles with love, lust, and betrayal and was one of the culminating productions in **KC MOlière: 400 in 2022**'s year-long activities celebrating his birth.

Secret & Lies set (Photo: Chantal Roberts)

Nicole cleverly recognized that in Molière's time, establishing oneself at court was the goal; today the same thing takes place on TikTok. Getting noticed, currying favor, flouncing and posing have always been prevalent – only the stages have changed. It is, after all, the timelessness of all of Molière's themes.

Despite having a raging headache, Chantal was charmed by the interpretation and adaptation. When her husband returned with a Diet Coke, she answered his question: "Yes, we've seen this play twice now. Once at Avila University in November and tonight." She was pleased he was beginning to recognize the themes, since he had readily admitted to being unfamiliar with her favorite playwright before the festival. She did not agree with the critics who disliked the fact the actors came out during the pre-show talk to tell the audience to turn off their cellphones.

Ridiculous, she scoffed. The actors' dialogue and gestures reflect Americans' current social network-focused lives and the role of "influencers." Celebrity is coveted and documented; "likes" rule. "Posting" is everything. Molière would be proud.

The final event in the yearlong celebration of Molière's 400th birthday was Kirke Mechem's opera, *Tartuffe*, undertaken by the new Landlocked Opera. Chantal wondered if the convenors of the opera planned the irony of the subject matter and the location. It was just another reason Molière was delicious.

Chantal, for her part, disliked opera, but Aaron had never been. She thought, perhaps a modern opera would permit

Chantal Roberts
June 10 · Overland Park · 🌐

One of the final productions of the festival celebrating **KC MOlière Jean-Baptiste Poquelin**'s 400th birthday.

Tartuffe—as an opera. Tartuffe, if you don't know, is a play about religious hypocrisy. Guess where it's being held.

In a church. 😂 I love Molière.

— at **Atonement Lutheran Church, Overland Park, KS**.

her to bear it; she and Aaron had had tickets to the Lyric Opera of Kansas City's production of *The Shining* in April 2020. Then, Mayor Lucas directed Lyric Opera to cancel the 2019/20 season due to the pandemic. So, when the world began to open up again, and because it was Molière, Chantal went to the production with an open mind.

Professor Anna Wheeler Gentry of Arizona State University, a former student of Felicia's, was the guest lecturer about the opera, which had been performed more than 450 times since it premiered in 1980 at the San Francisco Opera, making it one of the most performed operas by an American composer. Of course, it helped that Mechem also had ties to Kansas, giving the festival another tie to Molière and the Heartland.

Professor Anna Wheeler Gentry
(Photo: Felicia Londré)

"We can go if you like," Chantal said to her husband during one of the intermissions of the opera. The singing reminded her why she disliked this particular art form—although there are those who do enjoy it. However, her husband politely declined, much to her dismay.

Landlocked Opera Orchestra (Photo: Felicia Londré)

The lights in the church lobby dimmed to indicate that the performance was starting again, and Chantal found Felicia near the front of the stage, "I've thought about it, and I'll do it. I'll write the book."

Felicia again gave her little jump and expressed her tiny tell of joy. For four years, she and her small, devoted crew were Sisyphus pushing the rock of classical literature up the hill that is the love of all things modern and shiny. Felicia finally relaxed as she felt the Sword of Damocles removed from over her head, knowing she could step aside and enjoy this and any future Molière events.

Ce n'est « pas au revoir »
It's Not "Good Bye"

Even after the party, Molière's legacy lives on.

"I have the vivid memory of my mother having taken me, in Paris, for the first time, to see *Les Femmes savantes* at the *Comédie-Française* when I was 7. It's a very funny play, and for young French people to learn and know about Molière, I think, is one of the best (things); so, this is my memory," Cyprienne smiles, lost in the pleasant memory.

KC MOlière: 400 in 2022 hopes their educational objectives helped create fond memories for children in the Kansas City area who were treated to Molière through UMKC's Mobile Molière: The Long Path Players, *Tartuffenthrope!*'s public appearances, MoMo's interactions at festivals, and the numerous performances at area schools and universities.

Indeed, learning from history is what the classics are all about. **KC MOlière: 400 in 2022** has been incredibly blessed that UMKC's computer constantly fought with Felicia so that she created hard copies of all the organization's materials, which are housed in a couple dozen four-inch binders and soon will be safely ensconced with the framed copy of the City Council Proclamation in the Special Collections at Miller Nichols Library. Although, if the truth is known, Chantal is a bit disappointed that it won't forever live in Felicia's Office Maze, which so captivated her imagination four years ago.

Fortunately, MoMo will not reside in the library, although he would be a perfect tenant, as he is not very loud. Georgianna will keep the mascot for possible future appearances by unaffiliated groups, since **KC MOlière: 400 in 2022** was formally dissolved on September 29, 2022.

Becky confided, "Honestly, I was very little familiar with Molière up to my first meeting with Felicia and the arts representatives in town. Of course, I knew of him and his importance, and having him dropped in my lap that way spurred me on to read and experience him. Seeing how others revered him invigorated me and intrigued me. I also knew little of Kansas City's French origins. Then the idea of making the 400th a citywide, arts and educational, historic event was most enticing."

One lasting regret by the organization is that it could not do more for teachers in the Kansas City metro area to help them familiarize and invigorate their students with Molière. We can only guess what could have happened had there been no pandemic, no virtual school classes, and no restrictions on assemblies. As always, though, the Board had a backup plan, and the editor of the coloring book confirmed on August 2, 2022, the book's copyright and future royalties will go directly to KC Melting Pot Theatre. It's a win-win situation: for us, the coloring book remains in print. For KCMPT, it's a small (but steady, we hope) source of income.

It also seems many of the wonderful ideas and enthusiastic volunteers' work were left underappreciated by the public or hampered by the law. For example, **KC MOlière: 400 in 2022**'s Board felt it could not give more impetus to sales while it was an active organization, since that might have been seen as advertising alcohol. We hope that we, as individuals, can support master sommelier Doug Frost, who stored cases of *Joie de Molière* in his home, in the future. We were also forced to stop the engaging blog, on which Catherine Rush Thompson had worked so diligently, because of what appeared to be a phishing shakedown for money; however, one can never be too sure. The blog was converted to a *Jeu de Plume* site for publication of essays about Molière written by Rockhurst University students in Dr. M. Kathleen Madigan's advance French classes.

The caveats for other groups wanting to start their own nonprofit festivals and

use this book as a handbook is that care should be taken before engaging in and undertaking collaborations. Attorneys should be consulted first; royalty-free or volunteer-taken photographs used, permission obtained for use of written or photographic materials, even if the group is primarily an educational one and believes it can operate under the "fair use" rules.

Such groups should also have a fairly large war chest of funds to allow the organization to immediately begin tackling the expenses that come with the bits and bobs everyone must have to launch such a project – things like website hosting, postage for fundraising letters, and salary for administrative help. For example, the Fundraising Committee sent an appeal letter via USPS—we'd long assumed our emails were landing in spam because so many supporters swore they never received anything from us—with a cost of $229.35. It did bring in $4,056, but it was often felt we were operating on a shoestring budget.

Felicia Londré still shot from video by Amanda Davison and John Rice

"Molière flourished in the middle of the 17th-century and wrote about people he observed with all their flaws and foibles and problems. Well, we can recognize so much of what is in his work, because even though the costumes have changed and our manners have changed, people behave badly in a lot of the same ways," Felicia said with a smile.

"We can learn more about ourselves by looking at the past, and the classics are so fundamental to the arts, to the humanities, to everything about why we are here. So, I just think some kind of appreciation for the past would be a wonderful takeaway…in addition to learning something about one very great representative of the past: Jean-Baptiste Poquelin, also known as Molière."

Yet it seems even after a theatre troupe which can trace its heritage back to Molière, a French celebrity, French government officials' visits, and international press recognition of a festival for a long-dead playwright located in two fly-over states, our own mayor was unaware of the extent of what we did for our beloved city—through an ongoing pandemic—at no cost to him. When the mayor gave examples of Kansas City's world-class status at the opening of the remodeled Bloch School building at UMKC on Saturday, July 30, 2022, he failed to mention the people who had fallen in love with Molière and where the festival's campaign was hatched four years previously.

Perhaps Felicia can entice him to be a guest reader at the 401st birthday celebration.

Chronology of Accomplishments

Videos About Us

An overview of the **KC MOlière: 400 in 2022** festival's mission to produce art, theatre, music, dance, and culinary to honor the great French playwright, Molière, during the two and a half years around his 400th birthday on January 15, 2022. The festival theatrical presentations are included. Narrators are founder and festival president, Felicia Hardison Londré; past Honorary Consul to France, Cyprienne Simchowitz; and Matt Schwader Harbor and Hillary Clemons from The Kansas City Actors Theatre. The video was produced by Amanda Davison and John Rice. **http://bit.ly/3g6ym5K**

A 3-minute promo video by Amanda Davison and John Rice. **KC MOlière: 400 in 2022** is a two year citywide arts festival celebrating the 400th birthday of the great French playwright, Jean-Baptiste Poquelin or Molière. Theatre, film, dance, opera, music, culinary, puppetry, literary, and visual arts events include the Missouri Bicentennial anniversary fête for the French and Native founding roots of Kansas City, Missouri. The festival climaxes, but does not end, with a big birthday party, free and open to the public, on Saturday, January 15, 2022, 2:00 - 4:30 p.m., at the Nelson-Atkins Museum of Art. There will be birthday cake, guest artists, and celebrities, including our very own mascot, MoMo. Via YouTube site: **http://bit.ly/3OkldCl**

Hello Kansas City, video from the *Comédie-Française* to Kansas City, in French with subtitles: **http://bit.ly/3GkMh2H**

New Translations of Molière Plays And Molière-Inspired Plays

Professional Productions

The Miser (*L'Avare*) by Nicholas Henke

Blind Faith by Natalie and Talia Licardello

The Pests (*Les fâcheux*) a verse translation by Felicia Londré

Tartuffenthrope! Crossing Cultures with Chouteau and the Osage by Philip blue owl Hooser

Mademoiselle Molière written by Gérard Savoisien; translation by Felicia Londré

Secrets & Lies adaptation of *Sganaerelle or The Imaginary Cuckhold* by Nicole Hodges Persley

M de Molière by Jérôme Pouly

Academic Productions

UMKC *Mobile Molière*: The Long Path Players, directed by Stephanie Roberts, University of Missouri-Kansas City

The Precioius Young Ladies and *The Precious Young Men*, directed by Tracy Terstriep Herber, Pembroke Hill School

The Learned Ladies, directed by Chris McCoy, William Jewell College

The Imaginary Cuckold, directed by Matt Schwader, Avila University

Tartuffe, directed by Cinnamon Schultz, Kansas City Kansas Community College

The Imaginary Invalid, translated and directed by David MacKay, Kansas State University

The Imaginary Invalid, directed by Katheryn Bilbo, Northwest Missouri State University

Scenes from *Molière performed in French*, directed by Dorothée Werner, Académie Lafayette

Academic Translations

Chase-Scene Doctor (*Le médecin volant*) by Richard Rischar.

Publication and Dramatic Licensing

The Pests, a verse translation of Molière's *Les fâcheux* by Felicia Londré; Broadway Play Publishing.

Just for Amusement

Barbouillé's Jealousy (*La jalousie du Barbouillé*) by Chantal Roberts.

Our Book

Molière and France under the Sun King: A Coloring Book
Created by Kansas City artists to benefit **KC MOlière: 400 in 2022** (ISBN 978-0-578-90157-2); available from online booksellers and in the Nelson-Atkins Museum Bookstore. Contributing artists: Julia Brand, Kelly Brown, Georgianna Buchanan, Brigid Elbert, Sascha Groschang, Trudie Homan, Peregrine Honig, Karen Lisondra, Felicia Londré, Rebecca "Wes" Parrill

News About Us

July 2018

July/August issue. "Molière Festival to Celebrate the Playwright's 400th Birthday," by Rebecca Smith. *KC Studio*, page 22.

September 2019

23 September. "Molière Inspires Birthday Celebration in KC," by Bob Evans. *KC Applauds*. **http://bit.ly/3Xhdadl**

April 2020

April issue. "Make It Molière," *IN Kansas City*.com, p. 49.

June 2020

29 June. Beth Byrd-Lonski of the Visual & Popular Arts Committee was interviewed on KKFI 93.1 by Michael Hogge. **http://bit.ly/3TTltK2**

November 2020

11 November. "Molière Unites Chouteau and the Osage in New Play by Philip blue owl Hooser," by François Chouteau for the Native American Heritage Fountain website. Link unavailable at the time of publication.

February 2021

22 February. KKFI radio, noon to 1 p.m. Michael Hogge interviewed John Rensenhouse and Felicia Londré about *The Pests* on his Arts Magazine program. Link unavailable at the time of publication.

18 February. "Paying tribute to 400 years of Molière with *The Pests* in a dramatic reading," by Lucie Krisman. *The Pitch*, Kansas City's Independent Source for News & Culture. **http://bit.ly/3UBDmOB**

March 2021

5 March. International Relations Council video designed to win back a Sister City in France; Metz used to be Kansas City's Sister City. Tasha Zugazagoitia interviewed Felicia Londré, 10-10:30 a.m., hosted by Matthew Hughes. **http://bit.ly/3UToH1q**

July 2021

12 July. "Why *Tartuffenthrope!* at the Fountain?" Kansas City Parks and Recreation newsletter. **http://bit.ly/3EdO5HV**

16 July. KCUR 89.3 Morning Edition. Interviews on *Tartuffenthrope!*
http://bit.ly/3X8REbb

17 July. "Playwright Philip blue owl Hooser Creates a Comedy To Celebrate The Founding Of Kansas City," by Libby Hanssen. KCUR 89.3. **https://bit.ly/3X8REbb**

21 July. KKFI Radio, noon, Philip blue owl Hooser & Patricia Williams were interviewed by Maria Vasquez. **http://bit.ly/3TRMTjo**

22 July. "Philip blue owl Hooser's new work *Tartuffenthrope!* celebrates the city's bicentennial the birth of French playwright Molière," *Kansas City Magazine.* **http://bit.ly/3tJgiSb**

24 July. "KC MOlière: 400 in 2022 Presents *Tartuffenthrope!* by Philip blue owl Hooser," Cultural Services, French Embassy in the United States. **http://bit.ly/3Gwe14l**

August 2021

August 2021 issue. "Backstory: 1821," interview with Philip blue owl Hooser, *Kansas City Magazine*, page 120. **http://bit.ly/3AuEk7c**

September 2021

21 September. "Pastry, Wine, & Coffee as Art: The KC MOlière: 400 in 2022 Festival Introduces Limited Editions," by Bob Evans. *KC Applauds.* **http://bit.ly/3hNBOm0**

October 2021

11 October. "Culinary Art Just as the Sun King Intended," by Rachel Murphy. *IN Kansas City.* **http://bit.ly/3AvOxk1**

January 2022

3 January. "*Molière, un auteur 'au Panthéon des célébrités mondiales',*" *Le Monde* (Paris). Paragraph on **KC MOlière: 400 in 2022**, p. 23.

11 January. "THE PESTS with Dr. Felicia Londré," *Evil Thespian.* Apple podcast: **https://apple.co/3UQPNX2**; Spotify: **https://spoti.fi/3gmBU3Q**

12 January. "Director of *The Pests* Reflects on Return to Stage, KC Molière Celebration" by Emily Park, interviewing Matt Schwader. *IN Kansas City* **http://bit.ly/3hWXKLA**

14 January. "*The Pests*, Based off of '*Les Fâcheux*,' written by Molière, with a brand new adaptation and translation by Dr. Felicia Londré," *The Pitch* **http://bit.ly/3gsHEJ8**

15 January. "*400 ans de la naissance de Molière*," France Info Culture. This online article contains a link to the **KC MOlière: 400 in 2022** website: **http://bit.ly/3tlx6c7**

15 January. "*4oo ans Molière [1/2]: 'jamais là où l'on l'attend*'," by Siegfried Foster interviewing Martial Poirson. RFI (*Radio France International*). Kansas City gets a brief mention. **http://bit.ly/3V2WZ1U**

15 January. "*En France et au-dela, on souffle les 400 bougies de Molière*," *L'Express*. Kansas City gets a brief mention. **http://bit.ly/3GtcYCk**

Also, on France24: **http://bit.ly/3tlxhnN**

15 January. "A Guide to Exploring Kansas City's French Influences and History," by Libby Hanssen, KCUR's *Creative Adventure* newsletter. **http://bit.ly/3hSzeLD**

22 January. Kane, V. *KC Studio*. "Kansas City Actors Theatre Delights With New Translation of Molière's *The Pests*" **http://bit.ly/3u3VxB3**

24 January. Pivovar, C. *Kansas City Magazine*. "Theater Review: Kansas City Actors Theatre's *The Pests*" **http://bit.ly/3OmwfHu**

25 January. "Review: *The Pests* at Kansas City Actors Theater," by Lonita Cook. *Black Bee Buzz*. **http://bit.ly/3EkRg0J**

Janvier-février 2022

"*Molière: Les secrets d'un génie*," Special *Hors-Série* issue of *Le Point*. ISBN 978-2-85083-044-0. Mentions **KC MOlière: 400 in 2022**, p. 81.

4 January. "A Multifaceted Celebration of French Culture," by Vivian Kane. *KC Studio* XIV, 1 (January/February 2022), p. 27. **http://bit.ly/3AweXlp**

March 2022

15 March. Broadway Play Publications publication of *The Pests*, Felicia Londré's verse translation/adaptation of Molière's *Les fâcheux*, as premiered by Kansas City Actors Theatre **http://bit.ly/3GFrqXM**

24 March. "*M de Molière* by Jérôme Pouly," *Villa Albertine*, a newsletter of French Cultural Services in the USA: **http://bit.ly/3Xlodmr**

April 2022

25 April. Catherine Tissot and Felicia Londré on Michael Hogge's Arts Magazine show, KKFI 90.5FM, noon to 1 p.m., discussing the 400th birthday celebration and the visit of Jérôme Pouly. **https://bit.ly/3EvyZho**

May 2022

2 May. "Molière at 400, Kansas City MO," RFI English (Radio France International) video: **http://bit.ly/3XaPhVc**

2 May. "France's Molière Still Relevant in Kansas City after 400 Years," by Sarah Elzas, RFT (Radio France International): **https://buff.ly/3kwBtCp**

June 2022

8 June. *KC Studio.* "KC Melting Pot's Secrets and Lies Is a Wildly Creative but Ultimately Underwhelming Molière Adaptation," by Vivian Kane. **http://bit.ly/3XhKBwU**

8 June. "Molière's *The Imaginary Cuckold* reimagined at Melting Pot as a reality TV show with an all-Black cast," by Brock Wilber, *The Pitch.* **http://bit.ly/3VdUFVW**

10 June. "It's No Secret Nor Lie, *Secrets and Lies* Is FUNNY!" by Sun Beirutta, personal blog. **http://bit.ly/3EMWhAr**

Activities

May 2018

30 May. Kip Niven proposes our organization's name: **KC MOlière: 400 in 2022.**

21 May. Initial meeting of arts leaders to explore the idea of a Molière festival; 32 people attended.

September 2018

Publication of our first newsletter. Sent to about 500 email addresses.

January 2019

Publication of second issue of our newsletter to a growing email list.

May 2019

Publication of our third newsletter (Spring/Summer 2019). Eulogy for our founder, Kip Niven (d. 6 May 2022).

June 2019

June 18. Blog: "My Favorite Exploration of Molière's Comedic Genius," by Felicia Londré.

July 2019

kcmoliere400in2022.com goes live; Facebook and Instagram accounts open.

22 July. Initial Board of Directors meeting.

24 July. Blog: "One Dies Only Once, and Then for Such a Long Time!" by Rebecca Smith.

August 2019

6 August. Donor and volunteer party at Diastole generates approximately 40 volunteer sign-ups.

15 August. Blog: "How I Got Hooked on Molière," by Chantal Roberts.

23 August. 501c3 status granted by IRS.

September 2019

Publication of fourth newsletter (Fall 2019).

14 September. Blog: "Kansas City's French Founders—the Chouteau Family," by Catherine Rush Thompson.

October 2019

1 October. Blog: "French Connection: Learn About French and American Impressionists at the Nelson-Atkins Museum of Art," by Rebecca Smith.

8 October. Board of Directors meeting.

14 October. Blog: "French Farce-Comedy in the Spirit of Molière," by Felicia Londré.

November 2019

15 November. Dedication of land for François Chouteau and Native American Heritage Fountain, attended by Chantal Roberts and Felicia Londré.

15 November. Blog: "French Connection: Cyrano de Bergerac and Constant Coquelin," by Robert Gibby Brand.

December 2019

Publication of fifth newsletter (Winter 2019). Debut of our logo designed by Christina Schafer.

7 December. Blog: "National WWI Museum and Memorial: Enduring French Connections," by Jonathan Casey.

January 2020

6 January. Board of Directors meeting.

8 January. Blog: French Cuisine Has a Home in Kansas City by Catherine Rush Thompson

15 January. Molière's 398th birthday celebrated with Kansas City celebrities reading from his work at KC Melting Pot Theatre.

February 2020

Publication of sixth newsletter (Spring 2020).

6 February. Blog: "Celebrate Valentine's Day with French Flair," by Catherine Rush Thompson.

20 February. Don Dagenais and Felicia Londré represent **KC MOlière: 400 in 2022** at ArtsKC luncheon.

March 2020

11-13 March. Visit to Kansas City by French Cultural Attaché Tanguy Accart. Luncheon with Board of Directors on 12 March.

16 March. Summit Meeting on Zoom. Approximately 25-30 attended.

27 March. Blog: 'The Symbolism of the *Fleur de Lis*—Is This the Tattoo for You?" by Rebecca Smith.

April 2020

Facebook posts on **KC MOlière: 400 in 2022** page in April: 7 per week. 77 Instagram followers.

4 April. K-12 email blast sent.

6 April. Premiere of Book Club *The Imaginary Invalid*, Part *Un*.

11 April. Video 1 Five Minute Molière: *Why Kansas City?*

20 April. Book Club on *The Imaginary Invalid*, Part *Deux*.

23 April. Video 2 Five Minute Molière: *Molière Influences English Theatre*.

25 April. Bonus video in which Felicia Londré discusses *Le Malade imaginaire* (*The Imaginary Invalid*).

28 April. Video 3 Five Minute Molière: *Mademoiselle Molière*.

Kansas City Public Library lecture by Dr. Virginie Roche-Tiengo (School of Law, Sorbonne) scheduled for April, to be preceded by reception hosted by Gayle Krigel. Due to the pandemic, the lecture was re-scheduled for January 2022, and then re-scheduled again for 3 May. *See listing for* **3 May 2022**.

May 2020

May. K-12 email blast sent.

1 May. Blog: "*Vive Le Cocktail!*" by Rebecca Smith.

4 May. Video 4 Five Minute Molière: *Le Bourgeois gentilhomme* (*The Bourgeois Gentleman*).

12 May. Video 5 Five Minute Molière: *La Fontaine.*

15 May. Blog: "Exploring Molière: Cultural Enrichment through Digital Resources," by Catherine Rush Thompson

18 May. Book Club: *The Bungler* (*L'Etourdi*) translation by Richard Wilbur.

18 May. Video 6 Five Minute Molière: *Louis XIV and Molière.*

25 May. Video 7 Five Minute Molière: *Molière and Versailles.*

June 2020

Publication of seventh newsletter (Summer 2020).

1 June. Board of Directors meeting.

1 June. Book Club on *Dom Juan*, Part *Deux.*

1 June. Video 8 Five Minute Molière: *Back to Basics.*

2 June. Blog: "French Fairy Tales: Enchantments, Magic, Mysticism and Transformation," by Rebecca Smith.

8 June. Video 9 Five Minute Molière: *France's Financier Fouquet.*

15 June. Book Club on *School for Wives.*

15 June. Blog: "*Les Vacances*," by Chantal Roberts.

15 June. Video 10 Five Minute Molière: *Dom Juan.*

17 June. Bonus video in which Felicia Londré discusses *Molière Plays, Translations, and Adaptations.*

29 June. Book Club on *George Dandin*, Part *Un.*

30 June. Blog: "Ten Fun Ways to Celebrate Bastille Day at Home," by Catharine Rush Thompson.

July 2020

8 July. Philip blue owl Hooser commissioned to write a play set in 1821 about the Chouteau family and native nations at the confluence with Molière as a point of interaction.

13 July. Book Club on *George Dandin*, Part *Deux*.

15 July. Blog: "Keep Calm and Learn French—Where to Begin," by Chantal Roberts.

21 July. Blog: "The Miser Translator sees Modern World in Molière's Vision," by Rebecca Smith.

26 July. A collaboration between Sunday Script Circle and **KC MOlière: 400 in 2022** – *The Miser*, world premiere reading of a new translation by Nicholas Henke, presented virtually at 7 p.m.

27 July. Book Club on *The Miser* new translation by Nicholas Henke

August 2020

Publication of 8th newsletter, Vol. 3, no. 3 (Fall 2020). Call for volunteer artists for a Molière coloring book.

Facebook posts on **KC MOlière: 400 in 2022** page in August: 21. Events reach 348 people with 13 event responses.

1 August. Blog: "Measles and Louis XIV's Family—Who Survived?" by Rebecca Smith.

10 August. Book Club on *The Would-Be Gentleman* (*Le Bourgeois gentilhomme*).

15 August. Blog: "A Ghost in Silk," by Chantal Roberts.

18 August. Joint meeting of boards of Alliance Française de Kansas City and **KC MOlière: 400 in 2022** on Zoom to explore collaboration and mutual support.

24 August. Book Club on *The Pests* translation by Felicia Londré.

27 August. Event at François Chouteau and Native American Heritage Fountain; Keith Nelson introduces Philip blue owl Hooser and Felicia Londré.

September 2020

7 September. Book Club on *Tartuffe*, Part *Un*.

15 September. Blog: "The Influence of the Salons," by Felicia Londré.

21 September. Book Club on *Tartuffe*, Part *Deux*.

October 2020

1 October. Blog: "French Trading in North America," by Rebecca Smith.

5 October. Board of Directors meeting.

5 October. Book Club on *Les Précieuses ridicules*.

15 October. Blog: "Trappers, Traders, and Kansas City's French Bottoms," by Jeremy Drouin.

19 October. Donor appeal letter goes out to 419 addresses; cost ia $229.35; brings in $4,056 in new funds.

19 October. Book Club on *The Misanthrope*, Part *Un*.

26 October. K-12 email blast sent.

November 2020

1 November. Blog: "*Turquerie*—Fashion for All Things Turkish," by Rebecca Smith.

2 November. Book Club on *The Misanthrope*, Part *Deux*.

16 November. Blog: "With Just a Few Grains of This Salt, You Can Enrich the Flavor of Anything ~ Molière," by Rebecca Smith.

21 November. K-12 newsletter sent; also posted under Education drop-down on website.

December 2020

Winter newsletter (Vol. 3, No.4), our 9th newsletter, released.

1 December. Blog: "French Architects," by Chantal Roberts.

11 December. Email invitation from the office of the Mayor of Versailles to work with *Le Mois Molière* in Versailles, France.

15 December. Blog: "KC French Immersion Program Champions Adaptability and Academic Excellence," by Aaron Barksdale Burns and Catherine Rush Thompson.

January 2021

1 January. Blog: *"The Miser,"* by Rebecca Smith.

4 January. Board of Directors meeting.

15 January. Molière's 399th birthday celebrated with a Zoom party featuring Kansas City celebrity readings of selections from Molière's plays and the opening scene of Philip blue owl Hooser's *Tartuffenthrope!* Recording of the event and the program available on website under About drop-down *Enjoying Molière* and on the YouTube channel.

15 January. Blog: "Kansas' Mechem Gives Molière's *Tartuffe* the American-as-Apple-Pie Treatment," by Aaron Barksdale-Burns.

27 January. Blog: "Celebrating Valentine's Day with *Croque Monsieur* or *Croque Madame,"* by Catherine Rush Thompson.

February 2021

Spring 2021 newsletter (our 10th), Vol. 4, No. 1, released and archived on website.

Facebook posts on KC MOlière: 400 in 2022 page in February: 20

1 February. Book Club on *Lovers' Quarrels* (*Le Dépit amoureux*).

8 February. Zoom meeting with Julián Zugazagoitia, Anne Manning, Sarah Ingram-Eiser, Cyprienne Simchowitz, and Felicia Londré to discuss possibility of holding the 400th birthday at the Nelson-Atkins Museum of Art.

15 February. Book Club on *Amphitryon*, Part *Un*.

15 February. Blog: "Fly Me to the ... Forest?" by Chantal Roberts.

21 February. Unicorn's Thoroughly Modern Molière-commissioned new play *Blind Faith* by Natalie Liccardello and Talia Liccardello, 7:30-9:30 p.m. Zoom read by professional actors, followed by Q & A.

March 2021

Facebook page posts on **KC MOlière: 400 in 2022** in March: 25

1 March. Blog: "Louis XIV: His Influence on Childbirth," by Rebecca Smith.

1 March. Book Club on *Amphitryon*, Part *Deux*.

2 March. Higher Education Committee announces Molière production commitments from Avila University, Kansas State University, Kansas City Kansas Community College, Northwest Missouri State University-Maryville, Missouri Valley College, and UMKC.

7 March. KC Actors Theatre benefit of the world-premiere reading of *The Pests* by professional actors, directed by John Rensenhouse, via Zoom and available to watch for one week following. The event raises $575 for **KC MOlière: 400 in 2022**.

10 March. Felicia Londré gives her PowerPoint lecture on *Great Comedy from a Hard Life: How Molière Coped through Comedy*, 8:45-9:50 a.m., for Pembroke-Hill theatre class taught by Tracy Terstriep. $25 booking fee paid.

14 March. Blog: "Creating a French-Inspired Garden," by Catherine Rush Thompson.

15 March. Book Club on Richard Rischar's translation of *Chase-Scene Doctor* (Le *Médecin volant* aka *The Flying Doctor*).

15 March. K-12 newsletter sent by Dani Trebus to 700+ teachers. Deadline extended to 26 April for this semester's *Jeu de Plume* competition. As an attachment, Richard Rischar's new translation of *Chase-Scene Doctor* is offered for classroom use.

23 March. Board of Directors meeting.

29 March. Book Club on *L'impromptu de Versailles* with mini-lecture by Mechele Leon, University of Kansas Associate Professor of Theatre.

April 2021

12 April. Book Club on *Barbouillé's Jealousy*, a new translation of *La Jalousie du Barbouillé* by Chantal Roberts.

19 April. Contract signed for use of Kirkwood Hall in Nelson-Atkins Museum of Art for Molière's 400th birthday celebration on 15 January. Program planning begins.

21 April. Nathan Bowman is contracted to direct *Tartuffenthrope! Crossing Cultures with Chouteau and the Osage*.

22 April. Preliminary tasting of The Molière, a new pastry creation by René Bollier, Executive Pastry Chef and Chocolatier at André's Confiserie Suisse. David Weber of Messenger Coffee presents a cupping of various beans to blend an exquisitely paired coffee. René gives a tour of the kitchens for committee members Rebecca Smith, Doug Frost, Felicia Londré, and videographer Amanda Davison.

26 April. Book Club on *The Learned Ladies* (*Les Femmes savantes*).

May 2021

Release of our 11th newsletter, IV, 2 (Summer 2021).

10 May. Book Club on *The Doctor in Spite of Himself* (*Le Médecin malgré lui*). Last book club meeting.

16 May. A collaboration between Sunday Script Circle and **KC MOlière: 400 in 2022** – *Tartuffenthrope! Crossing Cultures with Chouteau and the Osage*, by Philip blue owl Hooser presented virtually at 7 p.m.

June 2021

1 June. *Molière and France Under the Sun King*, a coloring book created by 10 Kansas City volunteer artists, published June 2021, is available on Amazon and other online sites. ISBN 978-0-578-90157-2.

5 June. Kansas City Young Audiences. Teacher Appreciation and Season Announcement Reception. Debut appearance of MoMo. Launch of *Molière and France under the Sun King* coloring book.

7 June. Board of Directors meeting. Vote to add two board positions: Don Dagenais and Dorothée Werner as General Board members.

24 June. Beloved Vice President Sarah Ingram-Eiser passes away at KU Medical Center.

July 2021

1 July. *Blogging With Molière: 400th Anniversary Activities*, presentation by M. Kathleen (Katie) Madigan, with participation by Dr. Felicia Londré. American Association of Teachers of French, annual conference, on Zoom, 1 July 2021.

7 July. Board of Directors meeting.

8 July. Don Dagenais moves into the vice president position (open since the passing of our beloved vice president Sarah Ingram-Eiser on 24 June).

15 July. Jennifer Martin joins Board of Directors as a General Board member.

24 July. 8 a.m. to 1 p.m. Participation in dedication activities at François Chouteau and Native American Heritage Fountain: performance of *Tartuffenthrope! Crossing Cultures with Chouteau and the Osage*, MoMo, our mascot-head Molière, with flyers. Coloring book sales are brisk.

31 July. Board of Directors meeting.

August 2021

13 August. Kansas City Baroque Ensemble concert, composers who worked with Molière, **KC MOlière: 400 in 2022** kick-off reception follows.

20 August. Ethnic Enrichment Festival, Swope Park, Kansas City. 5:45-6 p.m. Photo ops with MoMo and performance of *Tartuffenthrope! Crossing Cultures with Chouteau and the Osage.*

August. Release of 3-minute promo video by John Rice and Amanda Davison, in production May-August.

September 2021

Release of our 12th newsletter, Fall 2021, Vol. IV, No. 3.

1 September. *Tartuffenthrope! Crossing Cultures with Chouteau and the Osage* nominated for Best Play in *The Pitch*'s annual Best of Kansas City voting. Voting open 1-30 September; winner to be announced in the October issue.

14 September. Felicia Londré's PowerPoint presentation on *Molière and The Learned Ladies for the Jewell Players* cast under direction of Chris McCoy, William Jewell College.

16 September. *Alliance Française de Kansas City* open house includes **KC MOlière: 400 in 2022** handouts.

16 September. K-12 e-blast to 700 area teachers of English, French, and dramatic arts.

29 September. Launch of *André's Confiserie Suisse*'s The Molière pastry along with Molière 400 blend Messenger Coffee and *Joie de Molière* dessert wine from Les Bourgeois Vineyards. Followed by pop-up events at Messenger Coffee and elsewhere.

October 2021

1-2 October. *Mobile Molière* public performances. The Coterie Theatre. The production then tours to schools until 15 October.

3 October. Board of Directors meeting.

4 - 15 October. *Mobile Molière* in schools, directed by Professor Stephanie Roberts. Pembroke Hill School (3:30 p.m. Oct. 4). Olathe High School with bussed-in middle schoolers and Q & A (9:30 a.m. Oct 6). Belton High School (9:45 a.m. Oct. 8). UMKC campus (7:30 p.m. Oct. 9 & 15). St. James Academy (11:20 a.m. Oct. 11). University Academy (9:20 a.m. Oct. 12). Frontier STEM (9: & 10:30 a.m. Oct. 14).

9 October. "Lit on Grand" at Afterword Tavern & Shelves. All-day event for local authors includes **KC MOlière: 400 in 2022**'s coloring book, *Molière and France under the Sun King*.

20 October. Felicia Londré's PowerPoint presentation on *Molière and Sganarelle or The Imaginary Cuckold* under the direction of Matt Schwader at Avila University.

21 October. Jennifer Martin's master class on Baroque period movement at Kansas City Kansas Community College.

22 October. Board of Directors meeting.

23 - 24 October. *The Precious Young Ladies* by Molière and world premiere of satirical afterpiece *The Precious Young Men* by Alli Jordan. Supported by a grant from the *Consulat Général de France*. Pembroke-Hill School.

November 2021

Release of Late Fall 2021 newsletter, Vol. IV, No. 4.

4 - 7 November. 7 p.m. Thur-Sat, 2 p.m. Sun. *The Learned Ladies* (Freyda Thomas translation) directed by Chris McCoy. Jewell Theatre Company at William Jewell College.

7 November. Board of Directors meeting.

8 November. "Molière as National Hero" lecture by Mechele Leon. UMKC Emeritus College Annual Dinner. Our 3-minute promo video by Amanda Davis and John Rice also is shown.

18 - 20 November. 7:30 p.m. Thur-Sat, 2 p.m. Sun. *Sganarelle, or The Imaginary Cuckold* (Richard Wilbur translation) directed by Matt Schwader. Avila University.

19 November. 12:10 p.m. Felicia Londré's PowerPoint lecture *Comic Genius at the Confluence: Molière and Kansas City*. The Shepherd's Center in Central United Methodist Church.

19 November. 6:30 p.m. Dr. Henriette Runte's lecture, Molière and Me, at the Kansas City Museum. **https://youtube.com/watch?v=wlPKh017878**

21 November. 3 p.m. Felicia Londré's lecture, *Sarah Bernhardt in Kansas City*, on Zoom and YouTube. Missouri Valley Sunday series, Kansas City Public Library. **https://youtu.be/8w8Ht2-2mdo**

December 2021

Jeu de Plume educational initiative: 17 essays by Rockhurst University students in Dr Kathleen Madigan's French classes posted on website until September 29, 2022: **https://kcmoliere400in2022.com/newsletters**

12 December. 7:30 p.m. Public reading of *Mademoiselle Molière*, by Gérard Savoisien, translated by Felicia Londré. Unicorn Theatre.

30 December. Board of Directors meeting.

January 2022

Release of Newsletter #14 (Vol. 4, No. 1).

15 January. Molière's 400th birthday celebration planned for this date, postponed by Nelson-Atkins Museum of Art because of staff shortages due to Covid. Event rescheduled to Sunday 1 May, 2-4:30 p.m., in Kirkwood Hall of the Nelson-Atkins Museum of Art.

15 - 30 January. *The Pests*, Kansas City Actors Theatre's world premiere of a new verse translation of Molière's *Les Fâcheux*, directed by Matt Schwader. City Stage in Union Station. 14 January preview performance; 15 January opening.

February 2022

5 February. Release of *Hello, Kansas City*, a short funny video in French with English subtitles, filmed at the *Comédie-Française* in Paris and featuring *sociétaires* of the C-F spreading amusingly garbled information about Kansas City, François Chouteau, and Molière. **https://bit.ly/3GkMh2H**

19 February. *Tartuffe* reading & discussion by Oak Hall play-reading group.

March 2022

3 - 6 March. *Tartuffe*, translated by Ranjit Bolt, directed by Cinnamon Schultz, Kansas City Kansas Community College.

8 March. Board of Directors meeting.

23 March-27 April. *Molière Then and Now*, a SPARK course. 1:30-3:30 p.m. on Wednesdays at 4825 Troost and online, by Dr Felicia Londré, Curators' Distinguished Professor of Theatre Emerita, UMKC.

Course Description

As theatres all over the world celebrate the 400th anniversary of Molière's 1622 birth with productions of his ever-popular comedies, Kansas City boasts a three-year buildup to the birthdate with play productions, lectures, videos, a coloring book, and even a pastry named The Molière. This course covers highlights from Molière life and work in the context of his time, the reign of the "Sun King" Louis XIV, when the arts encompassed both the Baroque and the neoclassical. Each session will include PowerPoint visuals and in-class reading of brief selections.

Wed. 23 March 2022

Introduction. **KC MOlière: 400 in 2022**. Overview of Molière's comedies and his place in world theatre. Scripts will be provided for reading *The Flying Doctor* during the session.

Wed. 30 March 2022

French theatre before Molière: farce, *commedia dell'arte*, tragicomedy, neo-classical tragedy and comedy. The *Hôtel de Bourgogne and Théâtre du Marai*s. Jean-Baptiste Poquelin before he was Molière. Molière's early career. Touring the French provinces. The Prince de Conti. Painters Nicolas & Pierre Mignard. The salons of Paris. Scripts will be provided for reading a scene from *Two Precious Maidens (Les Précieuses ridicules)*.

April 2022

Release of 15th newsletter (Spring 2022), Vol. V, No.2.

13-16 April. *The Imaginary Invalid*, translated by Miles Malleson, directed by Katheryn Bilbo. Mary Linn auditorium, Northwest Missouri State University,

21-24 April. *The Imaginary Invalid*, world premiere of a new translation by David MacKay of Molière's *Le Malade imaginaire*. Chapman Theatre. Kansas State University, Manhattan KS.

21 April. Presentation in French about **KC MOlière: 400 in 2022** by Trinity Hodges as her capstone project in Dr. Kathleen Madigan's class, Rockhurst University.

23 March-27 April. Molière Then and Now, a SPARK course. Continued from March.

Course Description

As theatres all over the world celebrate the 400th anniversary of Molière's 1622 birth with productions of his ever-popular comedies, Kansas City boasts a three-year build-up to the birthdate with play productions, lectures, videos, a coloring book, and even a pastry named The Molière. This course covers highlights from Molière life and work in the context of his time, the reign of the "Sun King" Louis XIV, when the arts encompassed both the Baroque and the neoclassical. Each session will include PowerPoint visuals and in-class reading of brief selections.

…

Wed. 6 April 2022
Pierre Corneille & *The Cid*. Nicolas Fouquet & Vaux le Vicomte. Court ballet and *comédie-ballet*. Molière and Louis XIV. Jean de La Fontaine. Scripts will be provided for reading a scene from *The Pests* (*Les Fâcheux*).

Wed. 13 April 2022
Madeleine Béjart. Molière's marriage to Armande Béjart. *The School for Wives*. *Pleasures of the Enchanted Isle at Versailles*. Molière's 5-year battle for *Tartuffe*. Scripts will be provided for reading a scene from *Tartuffe*.

Wed. 20 April 2022
Jean Racine. *The Misanthrope*. *Dom Juan*. Molière's friends: Boileau, Chapelle. *Le Bourgeois gentilhomme*. Jean Racine. Jean-Baptiste Lully. Scripts will be provided for reading scenes from *Phèdre* and from *The Bourgeois Gentleman* during the session.

Wed. 27 April 2022
The Learned Ladies. *The Hypochondriac*. Molière's death. The founding of the Comédie Française. Preparation for the Kansas City performance of *Le M de Molière* by C-F *sociétaire* Jérôme Pouly on 30 April. Scripts will be provided for reading a scene from *The Learned Ladies*.

29 April. 2 p.m. Performance of scenes from Molière by students of the Académie Lafayette International High School in the theatre at the Oak Street campus. Scenes from act 2 of *Les Fourberies de Scapin* directed by Mme Nora Abied. "Minuet" piano duo from *Le Bourgeois gentilhomme*. Scenes from Act 4 of *Tartuffe* directed by Mme Kate Absher.

29 April-4 May. Jérome Pouly, *sociétaire* of the *Comédie-Française*, in residence in Kansas City, sponsored by **KC MOlière: 400 in 2022** and the Alliance Française de Kansas City.

May 2022

1 May. 2-4:30 p.m. Free public celebration of Molière's 400th birthday (originally scheduled for 15 January but postponed). Kirkwood Hall, Nelson-Atkins Museum of Art.

1 May. 1 p.m. Matinee performance of *M de Molière* by Jérôme Pouly after which he joins the public celebration at the Nelson-Atkins Museum of Art.

2 May. 2:30-3:30 p.m. Jérôme Pouly in conversation with Rockhurst University and UMKC French students at Rockhurst's Arrupe Hall 212, hosted by Professors Kathleen Madigan (Rockhurst) and Gayle Levy (UMKC).

2 May. 5 p.m. Jérôme Pouly's Zoom from Kansas City to all branches of the *Alliance Française* nationwide.

3 May. 6:30 p.m. Lecture by Dr. Virginie Roche-Tiengo, Université de Paris-Sorbonne, on *Molière in World Culture* at the Plaza Branch of Kansas City Public Library (originally scheduled for April 2020, then for January 2022, but postponed due to COVID). Now available online on KC Public Library's YouTube channel.

15 May. 3:30-5 p.m. *Ensemble Correspondances* presented by The Friends of Chamber Music. Cathedral of the Immaculate Conception.

18 May. 9:30-11 a.m. CDT Zoom with Dr Henriette Pouly's two classes: Felicia Londré on Molière and French Literature, University of Hamburg, Germany.

June 2022

Release of 16th newsletter (Summer 2022), Vol. 5, No. 3.

3 June. Visit of Nicolas Douay, Higher Education *Attaché* from the *Consulat Général de France*, Chicago.

3-11 June. *Secrets & Lies*, a contemporary African-American adaptation by Nicole Hodges Persley of Molière's *Sganarelle, ou le Cocu imaginaire*. Kansas City Melting Pot Theatre.

9 June. Board of Directors meeting.

10 & 12 June. *Tartuffe*, the opera by Kirke Mechem. Landlocked Opera. Penn Valley Community College Theatre. Lecture preceding each performance by Professor Anna Wheeler Gentry, Arizona State University.

July 2022

14 July. Felicia Londré's PowerPoint lecture *Kansas City's French Heritage Salutes Molière* for the annual dinner meeting of the English-Speaking Union, Grand Street Café, Kansas City.

August 2022

5 August. Board of Directors meeting to begin process of dissolution. The meeting for the purpose of passing the Board resolution to dissolve the corporation and adopt and sign the Articles of Dissolution, 5 p.m. on Thursday, 29 September, at The Crestwood, 5401 Brookside Blvd.

Made in the USA
Columbia, SC
22 January 2023

75902534R00091